takes time

good food

neil perry
good food

photography by earl carter

styling and direction by sue fairlie-cuninghame

MURDOCH BOOKS

This book is dedicated to my beautiful daughter Josephine.
I know that one day you will enjoy vegetables.

Contents

Good Food starts with a couple of my favourite dishes for a good **brunch** — page 16. The **soups** are simple and delicious and make a great starter or one-bowl meal from **page 20**. The **salads** are great as starters, but also delicious for lunch or a summer supper — they start on **page 31**. Easy-to-make **pot pies** and a few any-time-of-day **egg dishes** start on **page 60**. The **pastas and rice dishes** are simple and even the lasagne won't take long; these are great for a midweek meal and they start on **page 67**. Some of my favourite **seafood dishes** start on **page 105**. Remember to get the freshest seafood you can find. **Poultry and meat** is full of classics and simple recipes. Go for gold with a simple midweek dinner or something a little fancier on the weekend; the recipes start on **page 149**. Afterwards, you'll need something a little sweet, so dive into the **desserts** from **page 214**. Knowing you will love the results of a little effort, you'll find all the **basics** from **page 238**. After that, happy cooking and enjoy!

Introduction

Good Food is all about beautiful, simple food to cook at home, to be enjoyed by friends and family any time. This book is not about special occasions but about celebrating good eating every day. I'm a professional cook and, as such, get the opportunity to hone my skills daily. But I'm also an avid home cook, where I like to make sure that food is simple, fresh and delicious. Take the stress out — that's very important. So, know that all these recipes are easy, but at the same time you would be glad if you ate food this good in most restaurants and cafés. If a recipe looks long, like the veal pie or lasagne, consider that it is just a few simple steps to fabulous food, so make the effort — it won't take much.

The idea for this book was born out of all the recipes that I cook and collect that didn't make it into my previous book, *The Food I Love*. In a sense, this is an extension of that book. In *The Food I Love*, I talk at length about good techniques that help make you a better cook every day. Use those techniques to cook the food that's in this book. Cooking is like most things in life — you get out what you put in. If you start with beautiful, fresh produce and bring out the best in it, with little effort you will have created something fantastic. These recipes come from a lot of my work with Qantas, magazines and television, as well as pan-rattling at home, so in other words, they are tried, tested and true and they won't let you down.

Take this simple philosophy into the kitchen with you for great results:

- Buy the freshest produce you can
- Buy the best quality you can afford
- Cook with the seasons
- Taste your cooking all the way through
- Season your food well — this is the main difference between professional and amateur cooks
- Rest meat and poultry before serving
- Most of all, cooking should be fun, so enjoy it and you will taste the difference.

This is not mandatory at all, but I believe my food tastes good because I use the following few things:

- Sea salt and freshly ground pepper
- Small packets of the freshest ground spices (or roast and grind your own)
- Quality extra virgin olive oil
- Quality balsamic and red wine vinegars
- Fresh lemon; freshly squeezed on roasts, barbecues and most fish dishes
- Quality Italian Parmesan cheese, freshly grated straight onto pasta and risotto
- Quality durum wheat pasta from Italy
- Organic chooks — so they taste like chicken should
- Organic eggs — I make so many good meals with this humble ingredient
- Quality meat, preferably dry-aged
- Beautiful sourdough bread.

If you follow my lead, I promise you a good dish will be great, and any effort put into cooking will be rewarded two-fold.

This book is set up to enable you to cook any of the main-style dishes simply, or add any vegetable you want. To that end I make some suggestions with many of these recipes, but by all means mix and match; use the vegetable dishes at the back to make a recipe change enough to keep your cooking fresh. One tip: make the harissa and keep it in the fridge. You will serve it on lots of braises, roasts and barbecues; it is a tremendous chilli relish that really brings food to life.

A word on pan-frying, sautéing, barbecuing, grilling (broiling), searing and roasting. They are all about cooking with heat, so if you like cooking your salmon or lamb chop on your George Foreman or Breville grill, then by all means do so. If you only have the old electric frying pan you got as a wedding present or that your mum gave you for finally moving out of the house, then use that — just heat it up and cook away. If you want to roast on the barbecue, then go for it. As long as you have a heat source to cook with, then great. Use the sauces, vegetables and garnishes and cook away any way you like; I'm not telling you what to do, I'm just helping you to get going, so happy cooking.

The most important word of all: with type 2 diabetes and child obesity such big problems in our society, strike back by trying to use this book and many others like it to encourage your children to eat fresh food. That is the key to these health problems. Processed food is full of sugar or salt, or both, which is what preserves it and makes it addictive. So encourage your children to eat fresh fruit and vegetables, to eat pasta with you, to like fish and to enjoy cooking with you. If we teach our young to eat well, it will stay with them all their lives.

Simple things cooked well at home are the future. Make a real burger and let your children know how good it tastes, cook pizza at home, take fresh fish and make little fish fingers, and make fresh juices to start the day off well. In the end, we can't help but blame ourselves if we don't set the right example. Life isn't about extremes — no fats, all carbs; no carbs, all fats, all proteins — it's about balance. Teach your children to enjoy fresh, flavourful food, and you will have established a very important part of making their lives better and richer.

Good food takes time; however, this doesn't mean that the recipes in this book are time consuming or difficult. It relates to the love of cooking, and is about taking the time to think about what you want to cook, recognizing the seasons, enjoying shopping for beautiful produce, and finally, experiencing the wonderful feeling that you get sitting down and enjoying good food with great friends and loved ones. Treasure these moments; they can be some of the best life can bring. This indeed is what *Good Food* is all about — the care and love of food.

Blueberry pancakes This simple pancake recipe is great to throw together for a lazy Sunday breakfast or brunch. To make maple syrup butter, just soften unsalted butter and purée in a food processor with maple syrup. Return to the refrigerator and spoon on the pancakes when they are hot. They don't really need anything at all, but trust me, you will love the combination and the effort is small.

150 g (5½ oz/1 cup) fresh or frozen blueberries
150 g (5½ oz/2 cups) plain (all-purpose) flour
2 tablespoons caster (superfine) sugar
2 teaspoons baking powder
1 teaspoon bicarbonate of soda (baking soda)
½ teaspoon salt
½ teaspoon ground cinnamon
2 eggs
375 ml (13 fl oz/1½ cups) buttermilk
125 g (4½ oz/½ cup) ricotta cheese
160 g (5½ oz/⅔ cup) unsalted butter, melted
  and cooled

Serves 4–6

Sift the flour, sugar, baking powder, bicarbonate of soda, salt and cinnamon together into a large bowl. Break the eggs into a medium bowl and beat until frothy. Add the buttermilk and ricotta to the eggs and beat well. Add the buttermilk mixture to the flour mixture and stir to combine. Stir in half the melted butter.

Heat a large heavy-based frying pan over medium heat and add a little of the remaining butter to the pan. Make two or three pancakes at a time by pouring batter into the pan, leaving space between each one, so they don't join.

Place some blueberries on top of each pancake and cook until bubbles form and the bottoms are golden; this takes about 2–3 minutes.

Turn the pancakes and continue cooking for another 2 minutes, or until they are cooked through. Repeat the process, adding a bit more butter to the pan each time. Keep the pancakes warm in the oven while you cook the remainder. Serve immediately just as they are — or with maple syrup or maple syrup butter.

Zucchini fritters with spicy tomato sauce These are beautiful little fritters that make a great light lunch, or simple entrée. They are perfect with some bacon and roast tomato for breakfast, or you can easily make a simple tomato and avocado salsa for them if you feel like something fresh, rather than the cooked sauce below. Serve with dressed lettuce on the side to make this dish a little more substantial.

250 g (9 oz) zucchini (courgette), trimmed and
    coarsely grated
1 small red onion, finely chopped
sea salt
3 tablespoons extra virgin olive oil, plus extra,
    to serve
1 egg
3 tablespoons plain (all-purpose) flour
100 g (3 1/2 oz/2/3 cup) soft feta cheese
1 small handful mint leaves, chopped
1 small handful dill, chopped
freshly ground pepper
crème fraîche

spicy tomato sauce
400 g (14 oz) vine-ripened tomatoes
1 tablespoon extra virgin olive oil
1 onion, finely chopped
2 garlic cloves, finely chopped
1/2 teaspoon ground ginger
pinch of saffron threads
pinch of chilli flakes
sea salt
1 handful mint leaves, chopped
1 handful coriander (cilantro) leaves, chopped

Serves 4

First peel the tomatoes for the sauce. Cut a small cross at the base of each tomato, and remove the woody core from the top. Plunge the tomatoes into boiling salted water for the count of 10, remove them with a slotted spoon and transfer them directly to a large bowl of iced water. This process will stop them cooking instantly and the skin will start to fall away, making them easy to peel. Peel the tomatoes and roughly chop the flesh.

To make the spicy tomato sauce, heat 1 tablespoon of the oil in a heavy-based frying pan. Add the onion and garlic and cook over low–medium heat until the onion begins to caramelize. Add the tomato, ginger, saffron, chilli and a little sea salt. Cook for 10–15 minutes, or until the tomato collapses and the sauce thickens. Stir in the mint and coriander leaves and adjust the seasoning if necessary.

To make the zucchini fritters, fry the onion and a pinch of sea salt in 1 tablespoon of the oil over medium heat until soft and lightly caramelized. Add the zucchini and sauté, stirring until it is soft. Set aside to cool.

Whisk the egg and flour together in a large bowl until smooth. Add the feta, zucchini mixture, herbs and a little salt and pepper, and mix until well combined. Heat the remaining oil in a large non-stick pan over medium heat. Drop heaped tablespoons of the mixture into the pan and fry until golden on both sides and cooked through. You should have about eight fritters.

Divide the fritters among four serving plates and top with some spicy tomato sauce, a dollop of crème fraîche and a drizzle of oil.

Pumpkin soup with a twist This recipe makes a nice variation on cream of pumpkin soup; the crème fraîche and spices add great complexity. If you want a really silky texture, push the soup through a fine sieve. However, it is good and simple just the way it is.

1 kg (2 lb 4 oz) peeled butternut pumpkin, cut into
    2 cm (3/4 inch) thick pieces
30 g (1 oz) unsalted butter
1 tablespoon extra virgin olive oil, plus extra,
    to serve
1 onion, finely chopped
2 garlic cloves, finely chopped
3 cm (1¹/4 inch) piece ginger, peeled and finely
    chopped
sea salt
1 heaped teaspoon ground coriander
¹/2 teaspoon ground turmeric
1 litre (35 fl oz/4 cups) chicken stock (page 245)
freshly ground pepper
crème fraîche

Serves 4

Heat the butter and oil in a large heavy-based pan over medium heat. Add the onion, garlic, ginger and a little sea salt and sweat over low heat, stirring occasionally, for about 10 minutes, or until the onion is soft but not coloured. Stir in the coriander and turmeric and cook for about 1 minute, or until fragrant.

Add the stock and pumpkin to the pan. Simmer gently over medium heat for about 25 minutes, or until the pumpkin is very tender. Remove from the heat and purée the soup until smooth. Check the seasoning. Divide the soup among four large bowls, dollop some crème fraîche on each, and finish with a good grind of pepper and a splash of oil.

Pappa pomodoro You must make this soup at the height of summer, when tomatoes are at their best. It can be made with tinned tomatoes but I prefer the subtle taste of fresh toms. I like to add a little more chilli sometimes. It also makes a great sauce for seafood straight off the barbecue.

1 kg (2 lb 4 oz) fresh ripe tomatoes, peeled, seeds removed and juice retained (page 19)
200 ml (7 fl oz) chicken stock (page 245)
125 ml (4 fl oz/1/2 cup) extra virgin olive oil, plus extra, to serve
8 sage leaves
1 tablespoon chopped flat-leaf (Italian) parsley
3 fresh small red chillies, seeds removed and finely chopped
2 garlic cloves, thinly sliced
1/4 loaf sourdough, sliced into 1 cm (1/2 inch) thick slices
sea salt
freshly grated Parmesan

Serves 4

Put the stock, oil, sage, parsley, chilli and garlic in a large heavy-based pan over high heat. When the stock begins to evaporate and the garlic begins to colour, add the bread. Fry over high heat until the stock is absorbed and the bread is crisp. Add the tomatoes and a little sea salt. Stir to break up the bread and cook for 15 minutes. Pour over enough water to loosen the soup, but keep it quite thick. Cook for a further 5 minutes. Check the seasoning and adjust if necessary.

Divide the soup among four heated bowls, drizzle with oil and sprinkle with Parmesan.

Chilled broad bean soup This is a simple puréed soup that would go well with salad and a loaf of crusty bread. Try making bruschetta by toasting bread, rubbing it with a clove of garlic and drizzling with extra virgin olive oil. Float that in the middle of the soup to really jazz things up. This soup is also delicious hot. Simply reheat the soup after it has been puréed, then serve it in the same way as the chilled version.

3 kg (6 lb 12 oz) whole broad (fava) beans
2 tablespoons unsalted butter
1 tablespoon extra virgin olive oil, plus extra,
    to serve
1 small onion, finely diced
sea salt
1 bintje (yellow finn) or other waxy potato,
    peeled and finely diced
1 litre (35 fl oz/4 cups) hot chicken stock (page 245)
200 ml (7 fl oz) cream (whipping)
1/2 bunch chives, about 15 g (1/2 oz), finely chopped
freshly ground pepper

Serves 4

To prepare the broad beans, remove the beans from their pods, cook them in boiling water briefly until just tender, and refresh in iced water. Slip the grey skin off each bean to reach the bright green inner bean. You should now have about 450 g (1 lb/2 1/3 cups) double-peeled broad beans. If you are time poor, you can substitute frozen broad beans.

To make the soup, melt the butter and oil in a heavy-based saucepan over medium heat. Add the onion and a pinch of sea salt and cook until soft. Add the potato, broad beans and hot stock. Simmer gently for about 20 minutes until the potato is soft. Add the cream and bring to the boil, then purée the soup until smooth. Place the soup in a large bowl, allow to cool to room temperature, then cover with plastic wrap and refrigerate until chilled. Check and adjust the seasoning if necessary. Divide the soup among four bowls, sprinkle with the chives, give a good grind of fresh pepper and drizzle with a little oil.

Spicy corn chowder This soup takes on an extra dimension if you stir through some crabmeat or cooked prawns (shrimp) at the end. A nice way to spoil some friends. Sambal oelek is a readily available chilli paste popular in Malaysian and Indonesian cooking.

4 ears fresh corn, kernels cut from the cobs, cobs reserved
1 tablespoon extra virgin olive oil
1 small onion, finely chopped
1 celery stalk, finely chopped
2 teaspoons finely grated fresh ginger
1 garlic clove, finely chopped
sea salt
1/2 teaspoon sambal oelek
1 teaspoon sweet paprika
1/2 teaspoon ground cumin
2 bintje (yellow finn) or other waxy potatoes, peeled and finely diced
875 ml (30 fl oz/3 1/2 cups) chicken stock (page 245)
80 ml (2 1/2 fl oz/1/3 cup) cream (whipping)
freshly ground pepper
100 g (3 1/2 oz/1/3 cup) sour cream (optional)
flat-leaf (Italian) parsley, chopped

Serves 4

Heat the oil in a large heavy-based saucepan or stockpot. Add the onion, celery, ginger, garlic and a pinch of sea salt and cook for about 5 minutes, stirring, until the onion is soft. Add the sambal oelek and spices and cook until fragrant. Add the corn kernels and reserved cobs (the cobs will release a starch that will act as a thickener to the soup), potato and stock and simmer, covered, for about 1 hour.

After that time, check that the corn kernels are soft. Remove the cobs from the pan and discard. Pour in the cream and bring to the boil, then purée until smooth. Return the soup to the saucepan, reheat and check the seasoning. Add some extra cream or stock if you wish, to thin the soup out a little.

Divide the soup among four heated bowls and give a good grind of fresh pepper. Add a dollop of sour cream to each bowl and sprinkle with a little parsley.

Note: I wouldn't normally use the sour cream if I were adding crabmeat or prawns to the soup.

Chestnut, pancetta and cabbage soup This soup is an absolute cracker — magnificent, wonderful and amazing; the list goes on. I love eating it at home with crusty bread and a salad. It is a truly hearty winter soup, and the best thing about it is that peeled chestnuts are available vacuum-packed and frozen these days, so with very little work you can make this beauty at home. If you like, purée the whole soup and it will still be delicious, but I love the texture as it is, with bits of nuts, cabbage and pancetta in the soup.

300 g (10$\frac{1}{2}$ oz) cooked peeled chestnuts
185 g (6$\frac{1}{2}$ oz) pancetta, diced
$\frac{1}{4}$ Savoy cabbage, roughly chopped into large pieces
2 tablespoons extra virgin olive oil, plus extra,
    to serve
1 onion, finely chopped
sea salt
3 garlic cloves, finely chopped
2 rosemary sprigs, leaves removed and finely
    chopped
150 ml (5 fl oz) full-bodied red wine
freshly ground pepper

Serves 4

Bring 1.5 litres (52 fl oz/6 cups) salted water to the boil in a large saucepan. Add the cabbage and cook for about 10 minutes. Drain the cabbage and reserve the water, as it will be used as the stock for the soup. Briefly refresh the cabbage in cold water, dry and then slice thinly.

If you are using fresh chestnuts in season, peel them carefully and boil gently in water for about 30 minutes, or until soft. Drain.

Heat the oil in a large saucepan and cook the onion and pancetta with a little sea salt over medium heat until the onion is soft. Add the garlic and rosemary and cook for a further 5 minutes. Break the chestnuts into small pieces and add to the onion mixture. Add the cabbage and stir for 1 minute, then add the wine. Bring to the boil and cook for a couple of minutes. Add the reserved cabbage water and simmer for about 15 minutes. Remove from the heat.

Remove half the soup from the pan and purée before returning to the pan. Reheat the soup over a gentle heat. Check the seasoning. Divide the soup among four large bowls. Drizzle with oil, give a good grind of pepper and serve.

Rustic gazpacho This wonderfully simple take on gazpacho is to be
eaten in midsummer, when tomatoes are at their height. More like a
salsa or a salad, it is great to eat with crusty bread. As it does resemble
a salsa, it is marvellous with barbecued fish as a little sauce.

500 g (1 lb 2 oz) vine-ripened tomatoes, peeled and
   seeds removed (page 19)
2 Lebanese (short) cucumbers, peeled and seeds
   removed
2 red capsicums (peppers), seeds removed
2 large red chillies, split and seeds removed
1 garlic clove
1/2 small red onion
1 small handful flat-leaf (Italian) parsley leaves
2 tablespoons good-quality red wine vinegar
3 tablespoons extra virgin olive oil
sea salt and freshly ground pepper
Tabasco sauce

Serves 4

Without going crazy, finely chop the tomatoes,
cucumber, capsicums, chillies, garlic, onion and parsley.
Mix all the ingredients together in a bowl with 3 tablespoons water and season well. Cover and place in the
fridge for at least 2 hours, but no longer than 4. Divide
the gazpacho among four large bowls and give a good
grind of pepper.

Cold roast beef, olive and cherry tomato salad with mustard dressing

You can roast the beef specifically for this salad, or you could use leftovers. I really like to barbecue the beef sometimes. It adds that smoky flavour to the salad, which is pleasing. A variety of tinned beans, peas and lentils are available out of Italy — these are really handy for salads, soups, pasta dishes and as side dishes with mains.

400 g (14 oz) cold roast beef fillet
8 Roman beans
250 g (9 oz) cherry tomatoes, halved
400 g (14 oz) tin cooked borlotti (cranberry) beans, drained and rinsed
60 g (2¹/₄ oz/¹/₂ cup) Ligurian olives
1 large handful rocket (arugula) leaves, washed and cut into julienne
sea salt and freshly ground pepper

mustard dressing
¹/₂ garlic clove, crushed
1 tablespoon red wine vinegar
1 tablespoon sherry vinegar
125 ml (4 fl oz/¹/₂ cup) extra virgin olive oil
2 tablespoons good-quality dijon mustard
sea salt and freshly ground pepper

Serves 4

To make the dressing, put all the ingredients in a jar with a tight-fitting lid and shake vigorously. Check the seasoning.

Slice the beef fillet across the grain. In a saucepan of boiling salted water, cook the beans for 8 minutes, then refresh in iced water. Cut them into slices about 1 cm (¹/₂ inch) thick on the diagonal.

Place all the salad ingredients, except the beef, in a bowl and toss together with three-quarters of the dressing. Divide the salad among four large plates, top with slices of roast beef and drizzle with the remainder of the dressing.

Salad of Roquefort, walnuts, radicchio and witlof

This is a classic bistro salad, perfect as an entrée or a lunch in itself, and so easy to make. It is important to get a good-quality blue cheese for it, as it really makes the difference. We are finally fortunate in Australia — after ten years of not being able to make this salad with Roquefort we now can, thank heaven!

150 g (5 1/2 oz) Roquefort cheese, crumbled
2 red onions, each cut into six wedges
extra virgin olive oil
sea salt
1 witlof (chicory/Belgian endive), leaves separated and washed
1 radicchio, leaves washed
2 firm ripe pears
2 lemons
freshly ground pepper
80 g (2 3/4 oz) walnuts, roasted and broken into rough pieces

Serves 4

Preheat the oven to 240°C (475°F/Gas 8). Drizzle the onion with a little oil, season with sea salt and roast for about 25 minutes, or until soft and caramelized.

Tear the witlof leaves in half, then tear the radicchio leaves into similar sized pieces. Quarter each pear and remove their cores. Cut each quarter into thirds lengthways and drizzle with the juice of half a lemon to stop the pears from browning. Place the leaves in a bowl and drizzle with oil and the juice of 1 lemon, add some sea salt and give a good grind of pepper.

Divide the leaves among four large plates and then scatter the roast onion, pear, Roquefort and walnuts over the leaves. Drizzle each salad with a little extra oil and squeeze some lemon juice on, as well. Give a last grind of pepper and serve.

Roast beetroot salad with goat's curd You can make this salad with fresh logs of goat's cheese and just cut the cheese into slices. However, the fresh curd is really delicious; it is the same cheese, just very fresh. Slow-roasted beetroot is incredibly sweet and worth the effort. Try placing some thin slices of raw beetroot that have been marinated in red wine vinegar and extra virgin olive oil on the bottom of the salad — the contrast between the two textures, raw and cooked, is wonderful. This is a great salad to serve as a starter.

4 beetroot, washed
extra virgin olive oil
3 tablespoons red wine vinegar
sea salt and freshly ground pepper
2 baby cos (romaine) lettuce, washed and dried
50 g (1³/4 oz/¹/2 cup) walnuts, roasted and broken
    into rough pieces
250 g (9 oz) fresh goat's curd cheese

Serves 4

Preheat the oven to 180°C (350°F/Gas 4). Lay a square of foil on the work surface large enough to wrap the beetroot in. Place the beetroot in the centre of the foil and drizzle with a little oil, 1 tablespoon of the red wine vinegar, a little sea salt and 2 tablespoons water. Wrap up tightly, place the parcel on an oven tray and roast for about 1 hour, or until tender. You can check the tenderness of the beetroot by inserting a knife or skewer into the centre of each.

Remove the beetroot from the oven and set aside to cool slightly. When the beetroot is cool enough to handle, rub all the skin off (it is a good idea to wear rubber gloves to avoid staining your hands); this should happen easily. Quarter each beetroot lengthways. Place in a bowl and drizzle with oil and a little more of the red wine vinegar, season with sea salt and give a liberal grind of fresh pepper.

Arrange the lettuce over four large plates, place four pieces of beetroot on each plate and sprinkle the walnuts over. Place a few dollops of goat's curd in the centre of each salad and drizzle with some more oil and red wine vinegar. Sprinkle with sea salt and give a good grind of fresh pepper. Serve.

Goat's cheese, lentil and potato salad This is very simple and delicious. I love lentils, but make sure you don't boil them, as it wrecks the texture. The wonderful earthiness of the lentils goes beautifully with the sweet cheese. I love this salad with a poached egg as well; make the yolk runny, so that when you break it, it will add to the richness of the salad. A meal in itself — the perfect lunch! Cooking the lentils first negates the need to soak them, so it is much more time-friendly. If you're really in a hurry, the tinned ones in water make a good alternative — just drain and toss, bingo.

240 g (8 1/2 oz) fresh goat's cheese, crumbled
250 g (9 oz) green lentils
2 bintje (yellow finn) or other waxy potatoes, peeled and cut into 1 cm (1/2 inch) dice
2 vine-ripened tomatoes, peeled, seeds removed and finely diced (page 19)
3 spring onions (scallions), finely chopped
1 large handful flat-leaf (Italian) parsley leaves, finely chopped
1 small handful mint leaves, finely chopped
2 garlic cloves, finely chopped
125 ml (4 fl oz/1/2 cup) extra virgin olive oil, plus extra, to serve
juice of 2 lemons
sea salt and freshly ground pepper

Serves 4

Bring the lentils to the boil in a saucepan of water, then remove from the heat immediately, drain and refresh under cold running water. Return them to the same saucepan and cover with fresh water. Bring to the boil, reduce the heat and gently simmer until cooked, but do not let it come to a boil, as it blows the lentils apart. Drain the lentils well and place in a bowl.

Steam the potato until tender, then allow to cool. Add the potato to the lentils, along with the tomato, spring onion, parsley, mint, garlic, oil and lemon juice, and mix the salad together well. Season with sea salt and freshly ground pepper, to taste. Divide the salad among four plates, top with goat's cheese and give a little drizzle of oil and a final grind of pepper.

Grilled haloumi with bread salad Haloumi, being a firm cheese, is great for this salad. You could also use goat's cheese, and instead of just dusting it with flour, you could crumb and shallow fry it. It ends up with a wonderful texture — crisp on the outside and melting in the middle. I love this salad served in the middle of the table for everyone to help themselves — great at lunch or dinner.

8 x 5 mm (1/4 inch) thick slices haloumi cheese
6 thick slices crusty bread, cut into 2 cm (3/4 inch) dice
1 small red onion, roughly diced
1 Lebanese (short) cucumber, roughly diced
2 large ripe firm tomatoes, roughly diced
100 ml (3½ fl oz) extra virgin olive oil, plus extra,
    to serve
2 tablespoons red wine vinegar
sea salt and freshly ground pepper
1 small handful basil leaves, torn
olive oil, for frying
plain (all-purpose) flour, for dusting

Serves 4

To make the salad, place the bread, onion, cucumber and tomato in a large bowl. Add the oil and vinegar and season with sea salt and freshly ground pepper. Mix well, add the torn basil and set aside to marinate.

Heat a little olive oil in a frying pan over medium heat. When hot, dust the cheese lightly with flour and add to the pan. Turn the haloumi over when it starts to form a crust and soften. Cook it in the same way on the other side. Remove and drain on paper towel.

Place the bread salad onto a plate and gently place the haloumi on top. Add an extra dash of oil and a grind of fresh pepper.

Crab and soba noodle salad with sesame soy dressing This is a classic seafood salad that would make an elegant dinner party entrée or a wonderful light lunch. You could exchange the crab for prawns (shrimp), scallops or lobster. It doesn't make a bad base for chicken either, and I like the combination of chicken and prawn together with these flavours.

250 g (9 oz/1½ cups) picked fresh crabmeat
270 g (9½ oz) packet dried soba noodles
1 red capsicum (pepper), seeds removed and cut into julienne
1 Lebanese (short) cucumber, seeds removed and cut into julienne
3 spring onions (scallions), thinly sliced on the diagonal
1 handful mint leaves, rinsed
1 handful coriander (cilantro) leaves, rinsed
1 teaspoon sesame seeds, lightly roasted
freshly ground pepper

sesame soy dressing
3 tablespoons sesame oil
1 tablespoon light soy sauce
3 teaspoons rice wine vinegar
1 tablespoon finely diced fresh ginger
1 garlic clove, finely chopped
1 tablespoon caster (superfine) sugar

Serves 4

Cook the noodles in boiling salted water until just tender, then refresh in cold water and drain well.

To make the dressing, place all the ingredients in a jar with a tight-fitting lid, seal and shake vigorously. Presto. Set the dressing aside.

For the salad, simply mix the noodles, capsicum, cucumber, spring onion and herbs together, and toss gently with half the dressing. Place the noodle salad in the centre of four serving plates. Divide the crabmeat among the salads, sprinkle with the sesame seeds and drizzle with the remaining dressing. Give a good grind of fresh pepper and serve.

King prawn cocktail It's a classic that just has to be done. Make your own sauce, get spanking fresh prawns (shrimp) and you'll understand why it's a winner: because it's so damn good! This is a dish that also looks great served in beautiful glasses.

16 large cooked king prawns (shrimp), peeled and
    deveined with tails intact
1 iceberg lettuce
extra virgin olive oil
sea salt
1 lemon
freshly ground pepper

cocktail sauce
3 tablespoons tomato ketchup
2 tablespoons grated fresh horseradish or 1 tablespoon
    horseradish relish
10 drops Tabasco sauce
250 ml (9 fl oz/1 cup) good-quality mayonnaise
    (page 246)

Serves 4

To make the cocktail sauce, simply fold the ketchup, horseradish and Tabasco through the mayonnaise until well incorporated.

Wash the lettuce and discard the outside leaves, then shred finely. Place some shredded lettuce in four bowls or beautiful glasses. Drizzle the lettuce with oil, sprinkle with sea salt and squeeze lemon juice over the top. Place the prawns on the lettuce and give a good grind of pepper, spoon the cocktail sauce over and serve.

King prawn and potato salad with gazpacho This is a 'great meal on its own' type salad — the gazpacho works as a dressing and a soup in one. Marinate the potato while it is still hot, as it will absorb lots more flavour that way. I also prefer them at room temperature, not straight from the fridge. Fresh herbs sprinkled over the salad are a welcome addition.

16 large cooked king prawns (shrimp), peeled, deveined and halved lengthways
2 bintje (yellow finn) or other waxy potatoes
extra virgin olive oil
sea salt and freshly ground pepper
50 g (1¾ oz/1 cup) rocket (arugula) leaves, washed
1 radicchio, leaves washed and torn into bite-sized pieces
1 lemon

gazpacho
2 teaspoons red wine vinegar
½ Lebanese (short) cucumber, peeled and roughly diced
½ red capsicum (pepper), seeds removed and roughly diced
¼ green capsicum (pepper), seeds removed and roughly diced
2 large very ripe tomatoes, peeled and roughly diced (page 19)
1 garlic clove, finely chopped
½ small onion, roughly chopped
½ large red chilli, seeds removed and chopped
2 tablespoons extra virgin olive oil
sea salt and freshly ground pepper
Tabasco sauce

Serves 4

To make the gazpacho, purée all the ingredients except the oil, seasoning and Tabasco until smooth. Push the mixture through a coarse sieve and stir in the oil and Tabasco, to taste. Season to taste.

Steam the whole potatoes until just tender when tested with a skewer. Be careful not to overcook them. Peel them while still warm, cut into 1 cm (½ inch) thick slices, then drizzle with a little oil and season with sea salt and freshly ground pepper.

Pour the gazpacho into four large serving bowls and carefully place the potato slices over the top.

In a small bowl, toss the rocket and radicchio together, then dress with some oil and the juice of ½ lemon. Arrange the dressed leaves over the potato. Now add the prawns to the same mixing bowl, drizzle with a little more oil and the juice of the remaining ½ lemon, season and place on top of the lettuce.

King prawn and chickpea salad with lemon anchovy dressing

King prawn and chickpea salad with lemon anchovy dressing You can take a short cut here. There are tins of chickpeas cooked in water available everywhere these days and they are very good. As a matter of fact, chickpeas, beans and lentils are great to have in the pantry. They make wonderful quick salads for lunch, such as here, are great added to braises, and will make a tasty sauce or purée.

16 cooked king prawns (shrimp), peeled and deveined
240 g (8½ oz) dried chickpeas, or 400 g (14 oz) tinned
    cooked chickpeas, drained and rinsed
4 garlic cloves
1 lemon, halved
1 celery stalk, quartered
1 bay leaf, fresh if available
sea salt

lemon anchovy dressing
3 anchovy fillets, finely chopped
2 garlic cloves, finely chopped
freshly ground pepper
100 ml (3½ fl oz) extra virgin olive oil
1 tablespoon lemon juice
1 handful basil leaves, torn
1 handful mint leaves, finely chopped
1 small handful flat-leaf (Italian) parsley leaves,
    roughly chopped

Serves 4

To prepare the dried chickpeas, soak them overnight in cold water, then drain. Put them in a deep saucepan, tucking amongst them the garlic, lemon halves, celery and bay leaf. Pour plenty of water over the chickpeas and bring to the boil. Reduce to a simmer and cook for 30–60 minutes (this will vary according to their age). Do not salt them until almost tender.

Meanwhile, to make the lemon anchovy dressing, mash the anchovies, garlic and a little pepper in a mortar with a pestle. Slowly pound in the oil and lemon juice, and finally the herbs, until you have a thick green slush. Check the seasoning.

When the chickpeas are nearing tenderness, add salt to the cooking water. When they are soft to the touch, drain them and dress them while they are still warm. Leave for at least 30 minutes to come to room temperature, then toss the prawns through and serve straight away.

BAROLO DOCG '00 PIEDMONT 149
ORI TIGNANELLO '01 TUSCANY 159
TORI del BARBARESCO '97 PIEDMONT 140
AMARONE '00 VENETO 132
AMARONE '01 PIEDMONT 140

LO GAVI DI GAVI '04 PIEDMONT 12/48 CE

ANO INSOLIA DOC 03 SICILY 8.5/35 SAN

ONI VERNACCIA DOCG '04 TUSCANY 11/46 TIE

O DI TUFO DOCG '04 CAMPANIA 62 DA

VALLEY CORTESE '04 VICTORIA 10/44 PI

ANI ROSE 03 VENETO 8/33 PO

FR

C

Smoked salmon and green bean salad with eggplant caviar This outrageously simple dish makes a very elegant starter for a weekend meal. It relies on the quality of the salmon, of course, so choose well. The eggplant caviar also makes a nice salad with hot smoked trout and a poached egg. That said, a plate of salmon with eggplant caviar and a poached egg on top isn't too shabby either. Use a very sharp knife to cut the chives, or snip with sharp scissors.

12 slices good-quality smoked salmon
16 green beans, trimmed
125 ml (4 fl oz/½ cup) extra virgin olive oil
juice of 1 lemon
sea salt and freshly ground pepper
½ bunch chives, about 15 g (½ oz), very thinly sliced

eggplant caviar
1 small eggplant (aubergine)
juice of 2 lemons
30 ml (1 fl oz) extra virgin olive oil
½ red onion, peeled and finely diced
2 garlic cloves, crushed
sea salt
10 French tarragon leaves, roughly chopped
1 ripe tomato, peeled, seeds removed and finely
    diced (page 19)
freshly ground pepper

Serves 4

Cook the beans in salted boiling water for 6 minutes, then refresh in iced water. Cut into julienne strips.

To make the eggplant caviar, peel and cut the eggplant into 5 mm (¼ inch) dice. As soon as you have done that, place the eggplant into a bowl with 500 ml (17 fl oz/2 cups) water and half the lemon juice. This stops it browning and keeps the caviar nice and white. Drain the eggplant and squeeze out the excess water. Steam for about 10 minutes, or until just tender.

Heat half the oil in a heavy-based saucepan and add the onion, garlic and a pinch of salt. Sweat over low heat until the onion is very soft. Remove from the heat. Combine the eggplant with the onion mixture, the remaining oil and lemon juice, tarragon, tomato and some freshly ground pepper. Check the seasoning.

Divide the smoked salmon among four plates. Dress the beans in a little of the oil and lemon juice and season with salt and pepper. Arrange the beans in the centre of the salmon, spoon the eggplant caviar over the beans, drizzle with some more oil, give a good grind of pepper, sprinkle with chives and serve. This salad is really nice to eat with thin slices of sourdough toast.

Salad of smoked salmon, avocado and roasted capsicum with salmon roe

Choose good-quality smoked salmon for this dish, as it makes all the difference. The salsa is good on grilled (broiled) or barbecued fish, and mixing the salmon roe in gives a nice explosion of flavour. The roasted capsicums (peppers) can be bought, but you can easily make your own by blackening the skin of red capsicums under the grill (broiler), or on the barbecue, then peel and marinate in extra virgin olive oil. Try to avoid running water over the capsicums to peel them, as it dilutes the lovely flavour. If mustard cress is a little tricky to find, you can substitute buckwheat sprouts or baby watercress leaves.

16 slices smoked salmon
1 avocado, stone removed
2 whole roasted red capsicums (peppers) (page 176)
1 lemon
sea salt and freshly ground pepper
extra virgin olive oil
1 small handful (about 4 tablespoons) mustard cress
2 tablespoons salmon roe

Serves 4

Using a sharp knife, cut the avocado and capsicums into fine dice. Place in a bowl and squeeze the lemon juice over. Add sea salt, freshly ground pepper and a little oil and mix gently. Arrange the salmon on four serving plates. Spoon the avocado mixture over the salmon, cut the mustard cress and sprinkle over each plate, then sprinkle with the salmon roe. Give a good grind of pepper and serve.

Chicken salad with my ranch dressing This is very easy and quick to make. Roast a chook yourself, or if you're feeling really lazy just buy one and bingo, a yum salad in a flash. Classic ranch dressing is usually made with dried herbs; I prefer to use fresh ones. You can make and use this dressing immediately, but it does improve with a day in the fridge. This salad is great for lunch, or perfect shared in the middle of the picnic rug.

1.6 kg (3 lb 8 oz) chicken, roasted
2 vine-ripened tomatoes, sliced into 5 mm (1/4 inch) thick rounds
1 avocado, stone removed and flesh sliced
1 cos (romaine) lettuce, washed and finely shredded
1 radicchio, leaves washed and finely shredded
extra virgin olive oil
freshly ground pepper

ranch dressing
1/2 teaspoon onion salt
1/2 bunch chives, about 15 g (1/2 oz), chopped
2 tablespoons chopped flat-leaf (Italian) parsley
1 teaspoon chopped oregano
2 garlic cloves, crushed
125 ml (4 fl oz/1/2 cup) buttermilk
sea salt and freshly ground pepper
125 g (41/2 oz/1/2 cup) good-quality mayonnaise (page 246)

Serves 4–6

To make the dressing, place all the ingredients except the mayonnaise in a blender and purée, then whisk the purée into the mayonnaise. Check the seasoning.

Remove the flesh from the chicken and cut into slices. You can remove the skin if you wish; however, I think that spoils the flavour of the dish. Place the tomato slices on large serving plates, place some avocado slices on top of the tomato, add the shredded lettuce and radicchio leaves that have been dressed with a little oil and make a mound in the middle of each plate. Place some chicken on the lettuce, drizzle generously with the dressing and give a good grind of fresh pepper.

Clockwise from top left: Chicken and herb salad with palm sugar dressing (page 50); Chicken and macaroni salad (page 51); Chicken salad with my ranch dressing

Chicken and herb salad with palm sugar dressing This is a classic Rockpool dressing that is easy to prepare and great with just about everything. Picking the herbs can be a bit of a bore, so get the kids to sit down after school and pick them for you. Use bribery if need be, as it takes all the work out of the dish and the herbs add a very sophisticated taste to what is essentially a simple salad.

2 chicken breasts, poached, or 1 roast chicken, shredded
300 g (10½ oz) bean thread vermicelli, soaked in boiling water for 5 minutes, then drained
2 Lebanese (short) cucumbers, halved lengthways and thinly sliced on the diagonal
1 carrot, cut into julienne
1 red onion, thinly sliced
2 French shallots, thinly sliced and fried until golden
250 g (9 oz/1⅔ cups) cherry tomatoes, halved
2 long red chillies, seeds removed and thinly sliced
1 large handful coriander (cilantro) leaves
1 large handful flat-leaf (Italian) parsley leaves
1 small handful mint leaves
1 small handful dill
1 small handful tarragon leaves
80 g (2¾ oz/½ cup) peanuts, roasted until golden
sea salt

palm sugar dressing
2 coriander (cilantro) roots, trimmed, well rinsed and roughly chopped
1 garlic clove
1 teaspoon sea salt
70 g (2½ oz) palm sugar (jaggery)
1 tablespoon sherry vinegar
1 tablespoon red wine vinegar
3 tablespoons extra virgin olive oil
2 tablespoons chopped coriander (cilantro) leaves

Serves 4

To make the dressing, pound the coriander roots, garlic and sea salt to a fine paste in a mortar with a pestle. Put the palm sugar in a small pan with a dash of water, and allow it to dissolve over very low heat. Continue cooking, swirling the pan occasionally, until the sugar starts to turn a rich golden brown colour. Add the sherry vinegar to the pan and cook for a further 2 minutes, then allow to cool. Add the red wine vinegar and palm sugar mixture to the coriander paste, then whisk in the oil. Add the chopped coriander leaves and check the seasoning.

Combine the shredded chicken, vermicelli and remaining salad ingredients in a large bowl. Dress with the palm sugar dressing and toss well. Divide among four plates and serve.

Chicken and macaroni salad This is awesomely simple, but outrageously delicious. So perfect for lunch or dinner just as it is. You can easily roast your own chook for this, but a good cooked organic one from the shop would be easier. You can remove the skin, but in a roast chook, that's where heaps of the flavour is. Finally, make sure you buy artichokes in olive oil; the ones preserved in brine are too strong.

1.6 kg (3 lb 8 oz) roast chicken, shredded
250 g (9 oz) macaroni or penne
2 celery stalks, cut into julienne
4 preserved artichoke hearts, thinly sliced
250 g (9 oz/1²/₃ cups) cherry tomatoes, quartered
2 hard-boiled eggs, quartered
125 g (4¹/₂ oz/¹/₂ cup) aïoli (page 246)
1 lemon
extra virgin olive oil
sea salt and freshly ground pepper

Serves 4

Cook the pasta in a large saucepan of salted boiling water, until al dente. Drain and refresh under cold running water.

Place the pasta, celery, artichoke, tomato and egg in a large bowl and gently fold in the aïoli. Divide among four plates and top with roast chicken. Squeeze over a little lemon juice, drizzle with oil and season with sea salt and freshly ground pepper.

Chinese roast duck and pineapple salad with cashew nuts and chilli lime dressing

This is a very easy Asian-style salad. You can buy a roast duck if you are passing by a Chinese barbecue shop or you could roast your own, or barbecue one — it is a great way to add another dimension of flavour, and I really love that smokiness the barbecue gives. Another option is to use quails; again, just throw them on the barbie. You could even buy a roast chook. All these options go well with the other ingredients in the salad … and have a look at what fantastic fruit is in season — lychees are wonderful with this recipe.

1 Chinese roast duck, flesh and skin sliced
1 sweet pineapple, peeled, cored and cut into
  bite-sized chunks
2 Lebanese (short) cucumbers, halved lengthways
  and sliced on the diagonal
10 cherry tomatoes, quartered
4 French shallots, halved and thinly sliced
90 g (3¼ oz/1 cup) bean sprouts
1 handful coriander (cilantro) leaves
1 small handful mint leaves
2 spring onions (scallions), sliced on the diagonal
sea salt
100 g (3½ oz/⅔ cup) cashew nuts, roasted until
  golden, roughly chopped

chilli lime dressing
1 garlic clove
3 wild green chillies, roughly chopped
sea salt
1 tablespoon caster (superfine) sugar
2 tablespoons fish sauce
juice of 2 limes

Serves 4

Prepare the dressing first. In a mortar, place the garlic, chilli and a pinch of sea salt and pound with a pestle until a paste forms. Add the sugar, fish sauce and lime juice to taste and stir to combine.

For the salad, put all the ingredients except the cashew nuts in a bowl, add the dressing and mix well. Divide the salad among four large plates and sprinkle with cashew nuts.

Prosciutto with tomato and bread salsa This is a yummy, simple dish that relies on the quality of the prosciutto. The salsa also goes well with other meats like salami or ham, and you can make a mixed plate as well, which is nice, or serve on a plate with a couple of other salads to make a lovely antipasto. To prepare the breadcrumbs, use a piece of stale sourdough with the crust on and chop it coarsely in a food processor — the texture of the crumbs is integral to the final dish.

16 thin slices prosciutto
extra virgin olive oil
freshly ground pepper

tomato and bread salsa
250 g (9 oz/1²/₃ cups) cherry tomatoes, halved
70 g (2¹/₂ oz/1 cup) sourdough breadcrumbs
1 tablespoon chopped flat-leaf (Italian) parsley
3 tablespoons tomato juice
extra virgin olive oil
red wine vinegar
sea salt and freshly ground pepper

Serves 4

To make the tomato and bread salsa, mix the tomato with the breadcrumbs, parsley and tomato juice. Add a little oil and red wine vinegar, then season with sea salt and freshly ground pepper.

Place four thin slices of prosciutto on each serving plate, overlapping them so most of the plate is covered. Spoon some salsa in the centre, drizzle with a little oil and give a good grind of fresh pepper. This is great served with crusty sourdough bread.

Lamb and rocket salad with black olive dressing
Here is a simple dish that can be served as an entrée or healthy one-plate meal. The black olive dressing is one that can be used on any number of other dishes to bring meat, seafood and poultry salads to life.

2 x 200 g (7 oz) lamb backstraps or loin fillets
sea salt
extra virgin olive oil
1 bunch rocket (arugula), about 125 g (4¹/₂ oz), rinsed
4 semi-dried tomatoes, chopped
freshly ground pepper

black olive dressing
10 kalamata olives, pitted and chopped
1 French shallot, chopped
3 tablespoons extra virgin olive oil
1 tablespoon red wine vinegar
1 teaspoon dijon mustard
finely grated zest of ¹/₂ small lemon
sea salt and freshly ground pepper

Serves 4

To make the dressing, combine all the ingredients and blend until smooth. Check the seasoning.

Season the lamb well with sea salt and drizzle with a little oil. In a very hot heavy-based pan, sear the lamb on each side for about 4 minutes, getting a good crust, before resting for 10 minutes.

In a bowl, place the rocket and tomato and drizzle with a little oil and season with sea salt and freshly ground pepper. Place some salad on each of four plates. Slice each piece of lamb into eight, then place four slices on each plate. Drizzle the olive dressing around the plate, with a little on the lamb, give a grind of pepper and serve.

Great with: Boiled and julienned green beans.

I often work day and night — that is the lot of a chef — but for me that can mean I live half my life in a chef's jacket, and the other half in a suit. Yes, this is the corporate nature of a modern chef's life. Even with all this going on I never lose the love of cooking at home and spending time with family. No matter how busy you are you must make time for relaxing over good food, good wine and most of all great company.

Winter vegetable pot pie

Winter vegetable pot pie This is a delicious vegetarian pie that can be made a day or two in advance and reheated when you need it. The filling can also be wrapped in three layers of filo pastry, rolled into a log shape and baked until golden and heated through. Cut into four to serve — what could be simpler? In this form it also freezes well for use whenever.

60 g (2^1/$_4$ oz/^{1}/$_4$ cup) unsalted butter
1 onion, diced
1 small leek, white part only, diced
sea salt
35 g (1^1/$_4$ oz/^{1}/$_3$ cup) plain (all-purpose) flour
125 ml (4 fl oz/^{1}/$_2$ cup) dry white wine
250 ml (9 fl oz/1 cup) vegetable stock
125 ml (4 fl oz/^{1}/$_2$ cup) cream (whipping)
1 tablespoon wholegrain mustard
1 tablespoon dijon mustard
40 g (1^1/$_2$ oz/^{1}/$_3$ cup) grated cheddar
20 g (^{3}/$_4$ oz/^{1}/$_4$ cup) grated Parmesan or pecorino
1 small swede, diced
1 parsnip, diced
1 carrot, diced
200 g (7 oz) bintje (yellow finn) or other waxy potato, diced
1 small sweet potato, diced
200 g (7 oz) cauliflower, cut into very small florets
150 g (5^1/$_2$ oz/1 cup) freshly shelled peas, about 350 g (12 oz) unshelled
freshly ground pepper
1 handful fresh herbs, such as parsley, chervil, thyme, sage and/or tarragon, finely chopped
1–2 sheets frozen puff pastry
1 egg yolk, lightly whisked

Serves 4

Preheat the oven to 200°C (400°F/Gas 6). To make the pie filling, melt the butter in a heavy-based pan, add the onion and leek with a pinch of sea salt and cook over low heat for about 10 minutes, or until the mixture is soft. Add the flour to the leek mixture and cook, stirring over medium heat, until the mixture is bubbling and grainy. Gradually stir in the wine and cook until boiling, then slowly stir in the vegetable stock and cream. Stir over the heat until the mixture boils and thickens. Remove from the heat and stir in the mustards and cheeses.

Blanch or steam all the vegetables except the peas until tender, then drain and refresh in cold water, then drain again. Add the blanched vegetables and peas to the cheese mixture, mix gently until well combined and season well with salt and pepper. Return the mixture to the stove and simmer over low heat for 5–10 minutes, or until the mixture has thickened slightly and the vegetables are just soft. Remove from the heat and gently stir though the herbs. Check the seasoning.

Spoon the mixture into four 350 ml (12 fl oz) ramekins and top with a round of puff pastry that is slightly larger than the top of the ramekins (the frozen pastry needs to be removed from the freezer 5–10 minutes before you want to use it). Brush the pastry with lightly whisked egg yolk and bake for about 15–20 minutes in the middle of the oven. Serve immediately with sweet onion relish (page 240) or your favourite relish or sauce.

Veal and paprika pie For a long time now, this pie has been off and on the Qantas menu, along with the lamb and pea pie. The great thing about the filling is that you can make it and use it as a sauce (just serve it with pasta, polenta or rice), or, if you like, instead of making it as a pot pie, wrap the whole thing in filo, about three layers does the trick, and bake yourself a serious pie. You can make individual pies or just one big one for the family. All you need is tomato sauce — I'd probably make that spicy tomato sauce (page 19) and a cold beer. Now that's a gourmet footy lunch for the boys!

700 g (1 lb 9 oz) trimmed veal shoulder, cut into 2 cm (3/4 inch) cubes
50 g (13/4 oz/1/3 cup) plain (all-purpose) flour
3 tablespoons extra virgin olive oil
2 tablespoons unsalted butter
1 onion, diced
2 leeks, white part only, sliced
1 celery stalk, cut into 5 mm (1/4 inch) thick slices on the diagonal
1 large carrot, halved lengthways and cut into 5 mm (1/4 inch) thick slices on the diagonal
4 garlic cloves, finely chopped
3 teaspoons sweet smoky paprika
1 bay leaf, fresh if available
375 ml (13 fl oz/11/2 cups) dry white wine
250 ml (9 fl oz/1 cup) chicken stock (page 245)
400 g (14 oz) tinned chopped roma (plum) tomatoes
1 small handful basil leaves, finely chopped
1 small handful flat-leaf (Italian) parsley leaves, finely chopped
sea salt and freshly ground pepper
1–2 sheets frozen puff pastry
1 egg yolk, lightly whisked

Makes 4

Dust the veal in the flour and shake away the excess. Heat 2 tablespoons of the oil and the butter in a large heavy-based saucepan over medium heat. Brown the veal in batches, and remove from the pan.

To the same pan, add the remaining oil, along with the onion, leek, celery, carrot and garlic and cook over medium heat for 10 minutes, or until the vegetables are soft. Add the paprika, bay leaf and white wine. Simmer, scraping any brown bits from the bottom of the pan, until the wine has reduced and thickened. Add the stock, tomatoes and their juice and half of each of the herbs. Return the veal to the pan and cook, covered, over low heat for 30 minutes, stirring occasionally. Remove the lid and cook for a further 60 minutes, or until the veal is very tender and the sauce has reduced and thickened. Stir in the remaining herbs and check the seasoning. Set the filling aside.

Preheat the oven to 200°C (400°F/Gas 6). Divide the pie filling among four 300 ml (101/2 fl oz) ramekins or pie dishes. Top each one with a piece of pastry large enough to hang over the edge of the dish (it is important to remove the pastry from the freezer only 5–10 minutes before you need it, so it thaws but stays chilled). Press the pastry down firmly around the edges of the dishes and brush evenly with the egg yolk. Bake in the middle of the oven for about 15 minutes, or until puffed and golden. Serve warm.

Lamb, mint and pea pie I love this pie. It was on and off the Qantas supper menu often. Then I decided it had to be a classic, and it is now always on the supper menu coming to Australia. Good things should always be around. The filling is delicious on its own, so don't hesitate to serve it as a braise with some rice or polenta, or even over pasta. In season you can use fresh peas, but at other times frozen work a treat.

1.25 kg (2 lb 12 oz) trimmed lamb shoulder, cut into
  2 cm (3/4 inch) dice
sea salt and freshly ground pepper
2 tablespoons plain (all-purpose) flour, plus
  1 tablespoon extra
80 ml (2 1/2 fl oz/1/3 cup) extra virgin olive oil
1 large onion, finely diced
2 1/2 tablespoons tomato paste (concentrated purée)
160 ml (5 1/4 fl oz) red wine
160 ml (5 1/4 fl oz) veal stock
225 g (8 oz) frozen green peas, defrosted
1 handful mint leaves, chopped
1–2 sheets frozen puff pastry
1 egg yolk, lightly whisked

Serves 4

Preheat the oven to 150°C (300°F/Gas 2). Season the lamb with salt and pepper and toss with the flour until evenly coated. Heat the oil in a large ovenproof heavy-based pan over high heat. Add the lamb in batches and cook for 1–2 minutes, or until well browned, then remove. Add the onion with a pinch of salt and cook over low heat for 5 minutes, or until softened. Add the tomato paste and extra flour and cook for a minute or so. Add the red wine and veal stock and stir until the mixture boils. Return the lamb to the pan, cover the pan with foil, place in the oven and cook for 1 hour, or until the lamb is tender. Stir through the peas and mint and adjust the seasoning if necessary.

Increase the oven temperature to 200°C (400°F/Gas 6). Divide the pie filling among four 300 ml (10 1/2 fl oz) ramekins or pie dishes. Top each one with a piece of pastry large enough to hang over the edge of the dish (it is important to remove the pastry from the freezer only 5–10 minutes before you need it, so it thaws but stays chilled). Press the pastry down firmly around the edges of the dishes, and brush evenly with the egg yolk. Bake in the middle of the oven for about 15 minutes, or until puffed and golden. Serve warm.

Asparagus, sage and Parmesan frittata This is a wonderfully simple meal — a great Sunday night dinner with a salad, some bread, a glass of wine and a good movie. If you have friends around you can cook a bigger frittata, or just make one after the other in the same pan; it takes about $1^1/2$ minutes to cook each one. Try any other kind of filling you like as long as it is cooked and only needs reheating. I like zucchini (courgette) and pancetta. Simply cook grated zucchini and pancetta together in a little extra virgin olive oil with a touch of sea salt and then add it to the egg mixture at the end. Yum!

6 asparagus spears, blanched and sliced on the
   diagonal
1 tablespoon extra virgin olive oil
2 eggs, lightly beaten
sea salt
2 tablespoons unsalted butter
4 sage leaves
35 g (1¼ oz/⅓ cup) freshly grated Parmesan
1 spring onion (scallion), thinly sliced
freshly ground pepper

Serves 1

Heat the oil in a small omelette pan. When hot, add the beaten eggs and as they start to set, drag the edge of the egg back to the middle, then add the asparagus and season with sea salt. What you want is for the egg to begin to set, at which point you then remove the pan from the heat to avoid overcooking. The residual heat will finish the cooking.

Turn the frittata out onto a plate, return the pan to the heat and add the butter and sage leaves. Meanwhile, sprinkle the frittata with Parmesan, spring onion and freshly ground pepper. When the butter is nut brown, spoon it over the frittata — the aroma is wonderful. Serve at once.

Simple Parmesan omelette with ham and cheese I had to put this recipe in because I just love omelettes, and so does my whole family. Just take some good-quality fresh organic eggs and you really can create a cracking dish. It takes little time and with a green salad and crusty bread, you have a complete and fantastic meal. The secret, if there is one, is this: have your butter foaming and starting to turn nut brown before adding the eggs — this is because it makes the omelette start to crust quickly — then don't overcook it, and bingo, the perfect omelette. You will need a fairly decent sized omelette pan to cook one this big; otherwise, make smaller omelettes.

8 eggs
extra virgin olive oil
2 tablespoons unsalted butter, diced
35 g (1¼ oz/⅓ cup) freshly grated Parmesan, plus
    extra, to serve
100 g (3½ oz) sliced ham, roughly chopped
75 g (2½ oz) grated gruyère
sea salt and freshly ground pepper

Serves 4

Using a fork, gently beat the eggs together with 3 tablespoons water, until just starting to amalgamate.

Put a large non-stick pan over medium heat and, when hot, add a dash of oil and the butter. When the butter is bubbling and nut brown, add the eggs and stir from the outside inwards, allowing the egg to set around the edge of the pan.

With the pan on a slight incline and using a spatula, pull the egg back from the side of the pan, allowing it to set as you go.

While the egg is still slightly runny, place the Parmesan, ham and gruyère across the centre of the omelette, with a little salt and pepper. Fold the first third of the omelette into the centre, then the last third over the top. Allow to cook for an extra 20 seconds, then turn the omelette onto a plate.

Sprinkle some more Parmesan over the top and finish with a drizzle of oil and a dash of sea salt and freshly ground pepper. Serve with a crunchy green salad.

Spaghetti with crab, tomato and raw fennel This is a very simple dish, and you can use any crabmeat that is available. If you really wanted to spoil your friends you could buy live mud crabs, kill them, break them up, steam them for about 8 minutes and, when cool, pick the meat from the shell. This then goes from being a really nice pasta dish to a sublime dish; a great one to fall in love over, so try it for that special new friend.

400 g (14 oz) spaghetti
200 g (7 oz) picked fresh crabmeat
2 vine-ripened tomatoes, peeled, seeds removed and
    diced (page 19)
1 fennel bulb, trimmed and coarsely grated
1 small handful flat-leaf (Italian) parsley leaves
1 small handful tarragon leaves
juice of 2 small lemons
2 lemons, segmented and chopped (page 83)
3 small red chillies, seeds removed and finely chopped
125 ml (4 fl oz/1/2 cup) extra virgin olive oil
sea salt and freshly ground pepper

Serves 4

Cook the spaghetti in a saucepan of well salted boiling water, until al dente, then drain and return to the pan. Add all the other ingredients, toss to just warm through, then check the seasoning and divide the pasta among four bowls. Sprinkle with a little sea salt and freshly ground pepper. I don't usually serve this dish with Parmesan, but you can do as you like.

Spaghetti with veal meatballs and tomato sauce

This is a classic dish that requires little effort. The milk-soaked breadcrumbs help lighten the meatballs. Working the meat firmly makes the meatballs stick together without using eggs.

400 g (14 oz) spaghetti
freshly grated Parmesan
freshly ground pepper

meatballs
350 g (12 oz) minced (ground) veal
25 g (2½ oz/⅓ cup) fresh breadcrumbs
2 tablespoons milk
extra virgin olive oil
½ small onion, finely chopped
1 garlic clove, finely chopped
1 tablespoon finely chopped flat-leaf (Italian) parsley
a pinch of chopped thyme
2 teaspoons tomato paste (concentrated purée)
2 small red chillies, seeds removed and finely
    chopped
1 tablespoon freshly grated Parmesan
sea salt and freshly ground pepper

tomato sauce
30 ml (1 fl oz) extra virgin olive oil
4 garlic cloves, thinly sliced
sea salt
800 g (1 lb 12 oz) tinned chopped roma (plum)
    tomatoes
8 basil leaves, torn
freshly ground pepper

Serves 4

To make the tomato sauce, heat the oil in a large heavy-based pan. Add the garlic and a pinch of salt and cook over low heat for 5 minutes, or until soft. Add the tomatoes and their juices and simmer, uncovered, for 20 minutes. Stir in the basil and check the seasoning.

To make the meatballs, soak the breadcrumbs in the milk until soft, then mash with a fork. Heat 1 tablespoon oil in a small saucepan, add the onion and garlic and cook over low heat until the onion is soft. Remove from the heat and cool. Combine the minced veal, mashed bread mixture, onion mixture and remaining ingredients and mix firmly until well combined and holding together.

Form the mixture into small balls. Drizzle some oil in a heavy-based frying pan and cook the meatballs in batches without overcrowding the pan. Brown on all sides and add to the tomato sauce to heat through. Meanwhile, cook the spaghetti in a saucepan of well salted boiling water, until al dente, then drain.

Divide the pasta among four large pasta bowls and top with meatballs and sauce. Sprinkle with freshly grated Parmesan and give a generous grind of pepper.

Spaghetti with clams, green beans, tomato and chilli This is a yummy variation on spaghetti vongole. I serve cheese with it — not the norm with Italians and seafood — but I just love it, so you decide. It certainly is good either way. Substituting mussels for clams is just as satisfying.

400 g (14 oz) spaghetti
400 g (14 oz) clams, washed
200 g (10 1/2 oz) green beans, trimmed
80 ml (2 1/2 fl oz/1/3 cup) extra virgin olive oil
2 garlic cloves, finely chopped
1/2 teaspoon chilli flakes
200 g (7 oz) tinned whole roma (plum) tomatoes, or very ripe fresh tomatoes, roughly chopped
sea salt
125 ml (4 fl oz/1/2 cup) dry white wine
1 small handful basil leaves
freshly ground pepper
freshly grated Parmesan

Serves 4

Clean the clams by giving them a quick rinse in cold water. Cook the green beans in a saucepan of salted boiling water for 10–15 minutes, or until very soft and starting to lose their colour. Drain and set aside.

Heat the oil in a large saucepan, add the garlic, chilli flakes and the tomato with a little sea salt and sauté for 5 minutes. Add the white wine and the clams, cover the saucepan and shake from time to time. It should take about 4–5 minutes for them to open (discard any that do not), then remove the lid and add the beans and basil. Check the seasoning.

Meanwhile, cook the spaghetti in a saucepan of well salted boiling water, until al dente, then drain. Add the pasta to the pan with the clams and mix all the sauce through. Divide the pasta and sauce among four bowls, sprinkle with grated Parmesan and give a good grind of fresh pepper.

Spaghetti bolognaise Here is another classic. It really is worth using both beef and pork; it adds to the flavour and texture. The bacon also adds great complexity and if you caramelize the vegetables really well, you will get even more flavour. Make this and serve it on toast if you want something easy. I always remember my father making lots of spaghetti bolognaise, and we would have the sauce for breakfast the next day on toast. Try it; it really is delicious.

400 g (14 oz) spaghetti
extra virgin olive oil
1 onion, finely chopped
4 garlic cloves, sliced
1 small carrot, diced
1 celery stalk, diced
100 g (3½ oz) smoky bacon, diced
sea salt
400 g (14 oz) minced (ground) beef
400 g (14 oz) minced (ground) pork
500 ml (17 fl oz/2 cups) full-bodied red wine
600 g (1 lb 5 oz) tinned whole Italian tomatoes,
    roughly chopped
2 sprigs thyme, leaves stripped and roughly chopped
freshly grated Parmesan
freshly ground pepper

Serves 4

Heat a little oil in a large frying pan. Add the onion, garlic, carrot, celery, bacon and some sea salt and cook for 15 minutes over medium heat, stirring occasionally. The vegetables should caramelize, but not burn.

Add the minced beef and pork and a little extra salt and cook for 5 minutes, stirring to colour the mince well. Add the red wine and bring to the boil, then simmer until reduced by half. Add the tomato and simmer for about 30 minutes. Add the chopped thyme; taste and check the seasoning.

Meanwhile, cook the spaghetti in a saucepan of well salted boiling water, until al dente, then drain.

Divide the pasta among four bowls, add the sauce, some freshly grated Parmesan and pepper and serve.

Pappardelle with duck ragu I love the richness of this dish; it is full of flavour and another one of those Qantas classics that works beautifully in the air. In *The Food I Love*, I give a version of this that is a little simpler. Here, I have marinated the duck overnight and I cook it on the bone, which I believe makes the ragu even more delicious. If you ever feel like making your own pasta, then this is a great dish to serve it with. It is really quite a wonderful thing to do, very tactile and nurturing. Like making gnocchi, it is quite simple once you have done it a couple of times … and by the way, this sauce over gnocchi is a knockout. It also makes a great pie filling, so get out the frozen puff and go for it!

400 g (14 oz) pappardelle
4 whole duck legs, about 900 g (2 lb)
750 ml (26 fl oz/3 cups) cabernet sauvignon or other
    full-bodied red wine
1 carrot, quartered lengthways, cut into 1 cm
    (1/2 inch) thick pieces
1 celery stalk, trimmed and cut into 1 cm (1/2 inch)
    thick pieces
1 onion, diced
6 thyme sprigs
1 bay leaf, fresh, if possible
1 small whole head of garlic, halved horizontally
sea salt and freshly ground pepper
1 tablespoon extra virgin olive oil
2 tablespoons tomato paste (concentrated purée)
3 tablespoons plain (all-purpose) flour
750 ml (26 fl oz/3 cups) chicken stock (page 245)
freshly grated Parmesan

Serves 4–6

Combine the duck legs, wine, carrot, celery, onion, thyme, bay leaf and garlic in a large bowl. Cover with plastic wrap and marinate in the refrigerator overnight.

The next day, strain out the duck and vegetables, and reserve the marinade, including the bay leaf, thyme sprigs and garlic. Separate the duck legs from the vegetables. Season the legs with salt and pepper.

In a large deep frying pan with a tight-fitting lid, heat the oil over high heat, until it smokes. Sear the duck legs for about 2 minutes on each side, or until well coloured. Remove the duck from the pan and set aside. Discard all but about 1 tablespoon of the fat from the pan. Add the reserved vegetables to the pan and sauté for about 5 minutes, or until browned. Stir in the tomato paste, fry for 1 minute, then add the flour and stir for a further 30 seconds. Raise the heat to high and add the reserved marinade with bay leaf and thyme sprigs and garlic. Stir to scrape any brown bits from the bottom of the pan. Bring to the boil and simmer for 5 minutes. Add the stock and duck legs to the pan. Bring to the boil, cover with the lid and leave to slowly simmer for 2 1/2–3 hours, or until the meat is falling off the bone.

Use a slotted spoon to remove the vegetables, herbs and duck from the pan. Discard the garlic, thyme sprigs and bay leaf. Continue to simmer the liquid for about 20 minutes, or until reduced and thickened.

Meanwhile, tear or shred the duck meat and skin. Discard the bones and cartilage. Fold the vegetables and duck through the sauce. Check the seasoning.

Cook the pappardelle in a saucepan of well salted boiling water, until al dente, then drain. Divide the pasta among the serving plates and spoon the ragu over. Sprinkle generously with grated Parmesan and freshly ground pepper.

Orecchiette with potato, peas and pesto You can buy pesto or make it in the blender, but I promise you if you pound it by hand it will taste so good you will never go back to the old ways. In *The Food I Love*, I speak about the necessity of having a mortar and pestle in the home. They are such great pieces of equipment and can be used for any number of jobs — from pounding marinades to making salad dressings, salsas and pestos … so do yourself a favour and get a good heavy one, if you don't have one already. I like using tinned peas in this dish — there are some sensational ones on the market and it makes the dish so easy.

400 g (14 oz) orecchiette
1 bintje (yellow finn) or other waxy potato, peeled
    and cut into 1 cm (1/2 inch) dice, boiled until soft,
    then refreshed in iced water
600 g (1 lb 5 oz) tinned peas, drained
juice of 1 lemon
freshly grated Parmesan
freshly ground pepper

pesto
6 garlic cloves
sea salt
50 g (13/4 oz/1/3 cup) pine nuts
2 bunches basil, about 200 g (7 oz), leaves picked
extra virgin olive oil
35 g (11/4 oz/1/3 cup) freshly grated Parmesan
freshly ground pepper

Serves 4

First make the pesto. In a mortar, pound the garlic and salt with a pestle. Add the pine nuts and pound, then add the basil and pound further. Add a little oil, followed by the Parmesan and freshly ground pepper, and then a little more oil. Check the seasoning.

Meanwhile, cook the orecchiette in a saucepan of well salted boiling water, until al dente, then drain and reserve 3 tablespoons of the cooking water. Put the pasta back in the pan and add the potato, peas, pesto and cooking water and stir until well coated. Divide among four bowls, squeeze a little fresh lemon juice over and sprinkle with Parmesan. Give a really good grind of fresh pepper and serve.

Orecchiette with pumpkin, broccoli and cauliflower This is so yummy; it is one of the braised vegetable pasta sauces I love the most. One of the reasons for this is the sweetness the pumpkin adds. You can also roast the pumpkin first if you like; it will introduce a nice caramelized character to the taste.

400 g (14 oz) orecchiette
400 g (14 oz) butternut pumpkin (squash), peeled
    and cut into 1 cm (1/2 inch) dice
100 ml (31/2 fl oz) extra virgin olive oil
6 anchovies
5 garlic cloves, sliced
1/2 teaspoon chilli flakes
sea salt
200 g (7 oz) broccoli, cut into florets
125 g (41/2 oz) cauliflower, cut into florets
freshly grated Parmesan
freshly ground pepper

Serves 4

Bring a large saucepan of salted water to the boil and cook the pumpkin until it is just tender. Drain and reserve the pumpkin. In a large frying pan, heat the oil and add the anchovies, garlic, chilli flakes and a pinch of salt. Fry for about 3 minutes, stirring continuously, until the anchovies start to melt in the oil. Add the broccoli and cauliflower and a dash more oil, cover, and slowly braise for about 20 minutes, or until the vegetables are well cooked and soft. Add the cooked pumpkin and check the seasoning.

Meanwhile, cook the orecchiette in a saucepan of well salted boiling water, until al dente, then drain. Combine with the sauce in the frying pan and continue to cook for a further minute.

Divide among four large pasta bowls and finish with freshly grated Parmesan and pepper.

Penne with scallops, radicchio and diced tomato

This dish takes no time to put together. The trick is to start cooking the pasta, then make the sauce. You should be draining the pasta (help is good) as you finish the sauce, then it all comes together and the scallops are not overcooked.

400 g (14 oz) penne
16 large scallops, cut into quarters
sea salt
100 ml (3½ fl oz) extra virgin olive oil
6 French shallots, thinly sliced
2 garlic cloves, crushed
½ teaspoon chilli flakes
1 radicchio, washed and roughly shredded
4 vine-ripened tomatoes, seeds removed and finely diced
2 lemons
freshly ground pepper

Serves 4

Cook the penne in a saucepan of well salted boiling water, until al dente, then drain.

Meanwhile, sprinkle the scallops with sea salt. Heat 1 tablespoon of the oil in a heavy-based saucepan, add the shallots, garlic and chilli and cook for 1 minute. Add the scallops and fry until just sealed, then add the radicchio, tomato and the remainder of the oil. Quickly remove the saucepan from the heat, add the pasta and mix through.

Divide among four large pasta bowls, squeeze the juice of ½ lemon over each and give a generous grind of pepper.

Tagliatelle with rocket, lemon and chilli

Simple and delicious, this dish is really just pasta tossed through vinaigrette. Make it as hot as you like — the chilli hit with the lemon is really good — and you can exchange the rocket for other herbs if you prefer, but the pepper flavour works very well.

400 g (14 oz) tagliatelle
3 lemons
2 bunches rocket (arugula), about 250 g (9 oz), rinsed
4 fresh red chillies, seeds removed and finely diced
3 anchovies, finely chopped
100 ml (3¹/₂ fl oz) extra virgin olive oil
juice of 2 lemons
sea salt and freshly ground pepper
freshly grated Parmesan

Serves 4

First segment the lemons. To do this, cut away both ends of the lemon so you can see the flesh and sit it flat on a chopping board, then, working down, cut the skin off, from top to bottom, working around the lemon until all the skin and pith has gone. Cut just inside a membrane to the middle of the lemon, repeat on the other side and the segment should fall out. Have a little bowl ready to catch the segments, then, when you have finished, squeeze the lemon to get any juice that is left.

Pick the leaves off the rocket and shred, then place in the bowl with the lemon segments. Add the chilli, anchovies, oil and lemon juice and stir gently. Season with sea salt and freshly ground pepper, taste and adjust the seasoning if necessary.

Cook the tagliatelle in a saucepan of well salted boiling water, until al dente. Drain, but leave a little cooking water still clinging to the pasta to keep it moist. Quickly add it to the bowl with the other ingredients and toss together well. Divide among four large pasta bowls. Sprinkle with freshly grated Parmesan and give a generous grind of fresh pepper. Serve immediately.

Fusilli with squid and tomato There are two ways to cook squid: briefly, so it is tender and full of the flavour of the sea, and long braised, where it becomes meltingly tender and the flavour deepens. I love it both ways. Again, I like this seafood dish with Parmesan cheese — very un-Italian, but it tastes great. So you do as you please.

400 g (14 oz) fusilli
400 g (14 oz) cleaned squid tubes, opened up and
    cut into 2 cm (3/4 inch) thick slices
80 ml (21/2 fl oz/1/3 cup) extra virgin olive oil
2 small carrots, cut into 5 mm (1/4 inch) thick slices
1 small leek, cut into 1 cm (1/2 inch) thick slices,
    well rinsed
1 onion, cut into 1 cm (1/2 inch) dice
3 garlic cloves, finely chopped
1/2 teaspoon chilli flakes
sea salt
400 g (14 oz) tinned tomatoes, puréed
3 tablespoons red wine vinegar
250 ml (9 fl oz/1 cup) red wine
2 teaspoons salted baby capers, rinsed
1 handful flat-leaf (Italian) parsley leaves,
    roughly chopped
freshly grated Parmesan (optional)
freshly ground pepper

Serves 4

Heat the oil in a heavy-based saucepan. Add the carrot, leek, onion, garlic, chilli flakes and a little salt and cook slowly for about 10 minutes. Add the squid and cook for a further 3 minutes.

Pour in the puréed tomato, vinegar and wine and braise for 1 hour, uncovered. Add the capers and parsley and check the seasoning.

Meanwhile, cook the fusilli in a saucepan of well salted boiling water, until al dente, then drain.

Divide the pasta among four large pasta bowls and spoon the sauce over the top. Sprinkle with grated Parmesan and give a generous grind of fresh pepper.

Best-ever lasagne This is quick and easy and wonderful. The vinegar really lifts the taste and the extra tomato keeps it moist and full of flavour. Passata is a smooth tomato sauce, available at your local deli. Don't think of this as a long recipe, think of it like this: make a meat sauce, make a béchamel, grate some cheese and put it together — it really is that simple.

9 instant-cook lasagne sheets
500 g (1 lb 2 oz) fresh buffalo or cow's milk
    mozzarella, torn
100 g (3½ oz/1 cup) freshly grated Parmesan

meat sauce
1 tablespoon extra virgin olive oil
1 onion, finely chopped
6 garlic cloves, finely chopped
300 g (10½ oz) pork mince
300 g (10½ oz) veal mince
sea salt and freshly ground pepper
2 teaspoons plain (all-purpose) flour
2 tablespoons balsamic vinegar
a pinch of caster (superfine) sugar
700 ml (24 fl oz) tomato passata (puréed tomatoes)
400 g (14 oz) tinned diced tomatoes
1 large handful basil leaves

béchamel sauce
50 g (1¾ oz) unsalted butter
2 tablespoons plain (all-purpose) flour
600 ml (21 fl oz) milk
sea salt and freshly ground pepper

Serves 6

You will require a 23 x 29 x 7 cm (9 x 11½ x 2¾ inch) lasagne dish. Adjust the oven rack to the middle position and preheat the oven to 190°C (375°F/Gas 5).

To make the meat sauce, heat the oil in a large heavy-based frying pan over medium heat. Add the onion and cook, stirring occasionally, until softened but not browned. Add the garlic and cook until fragrant. Increase the heat to medium–high and add both of the meats and a pinch of salt and pepper. Cook, breaking the meat into small pieces with a wooden spoon, for about 4 minutes, or until the meat loses its raw colour but has not browned. Add the flour and cook, stirring, for 2 minutes, then pour in the vinegar and stir occasionally until it has almost completely evaporated. Add the sugar, passata and diced tomatoes and allow the sauce to simmer for about 10 minutes, or until it reduces and thickens slightly. Adjust the seasoning, stir through the basil leaves and set the sauce aside (at this stage, the sauce can be cooled, covered and refrigerated for up to two days, then reheated before assembling the lasagne).

To make the béchamel sauce, melt the butter in a heavy-based saucepan over low–medium heat. Add the flour to the butter and stir constantly over the heat, for 1–2 minutes. Remove the pan from the heat and add the milk all at once, whisking constantly, to avoid any lumps. Return the pan to the heat and continue to whisk constantly, until the sauce boils and thickens. Remove from the heat and season with salt and pepper.

To assemble the lasagne, spread one-quarter of the meat sauce into the base of the lasagne dish. Place three of the lasagne sheets over the sauce. Spread another quarter of the sauce over the lasagne sheets, followed by one-third of the mozzarella. Continue to layer the lasagne sheets, sauce and mozzarella two more times. Pour the béchamel sauce evenly over the final layer of mozzarella, then sprinkle evenly with Parmesan. Cook the lasagne for 30 minutes, or until the cheese has browned and the sauce is bubbling. Remove the lasagne from the oven and let it stand at room temperature for 10 minutes before serving.

Ricotta and spinach gnocchi with burnt butter
This type of gnocchi is lighter than potato gnocchi. Make sure you squeeze as much liquid out of the spinach as possible. The gnocchi is also fantastic with king prawns (shrimp), lightly sautéed and placed on top.

4 bunches English spinach, about 1 kg (2 lb 4 oz), trimmed and washed well
350 g (12 oz) ricotta cheese
3 tablespoons freshly grated Parmesan, plus extra, to serve
2 egg yolks, lightly beaten
sea salt and freshly ground pepper
plain (all-purpose) flour, for dusting
100 g (3½ oz) unsalted butter
16 sage leaves

Serves 4

Blanch the spinach in boiling water until just wilted, then drain, plunge into iced water and drain again. Squeeze out as much liquid as possible, then chop finely and put into a bowl. Add the ricotta, Parmesan and the egg yolks and season with salt and pepper to taste. Roll level tablespoons of the mixture into balls, place on a tray and refrigerate for 20 minutes.

Bring a large saucepan of lightly salted water to a gentle boil. Remove the gnocchi from the refrigerator and lightly dust with flour. Add the gnocchi to the water, a few at a time, and remove with a slotted spoon as they rise to the surface. Divide the gnocchi among four bowls and sprinkle liberally with Parmesan and freshly ground pepper.

Meanwhile, put the butter into a frying pan with the sage leaves and heat until the butter turns nut brown. Spoon the butter and sage over the gnocchi and serve immediately.

Pumpkin, sweet potato, pea and chilli risotto Like other risottos in this book, this one also uses the water for cooking the vegetables as the stock. I have deliberately kept the dish vegetarian, and this method is easier than making your own chicken stock. However, if you want to, you can use 1 litre (35 fl oz/4 cups) chicken stock (page 245); it will add a little more body and complexity of flavour to the dish. Importantly, don't replace fresh chicken stock with those concentrates that are shelf stable. Bloody horrible is the only term for them — you will end up with the taste of your risotto completely dominated by it!

220 g (7³/4 oz/1 cup) arborio rice
60 g (2¹/4 oz) unsalted butter
200 g (7 oz) pumpkin (winter squash), cut into 1 cm (¹/2 inch) dice
200 g (7 oz) sweet potato, cut into 1 cm (¹/2 inch) dice
150 g (5¹/2 oz/1 cup) freshly shelled peas, about 350 g (12 oz) unshelled
extra virgin olive oil
¹/2 onion, finely diced
2 garlic cloves, finely chopped
2 small red chillies, seeds removed and finely diced
¹/2 teaspoon chilli flakes
sea salt
80 ml (2¹/2 fl oz/¹/3 cup) dry white wine
1 small handful basil leaves, roughly chopped
35 g (1¹/4 oz/¹/3 cup) freshly grated Parmesan, plus extra, to serve
freshly ground pepper

Serves 4

Heat 2 litres (70 fl oz/8 cups) salted water with half the butter in a saucepan and bring to the boil. Add the pumpkin and sweet potato and cook for 10 minutes until soft, then remove and set aside. Cook the peas in the same water for about 5 minutes, then remove and place into iced water. Remove from the water when cool. Reserve the cooking liquid — you will need about 1 litre (35 fl oz/4 cups) — and keep hot.

In a heavy-based frying pan, melt some of the remaining butter in a little oil and cook the onion, garlic, chilli, chilli flakes and a little salt over low heat until translucent. Add the rice and stir continuously until it starts to stick. Pour in the wine and allow it to reduce completely, then add ladle after ladle of the hot reserved cooking liquid, stirring all the time and allowing each ladle to be absorbed before you add the next. Be careful not to drown the rice or allow it to dry out. Repeat this process for 15–18 minutes until the rice grains are soft but with a firm bite.

With the last two ladles of stock, add the pumpkin, sweet potato, peas, basil, Parmesan and remaining butter and stir through. Check the seasoning. Rest the risotto for 1 minute. Divide among four large pasta bowls, add the extra Parmesan and some freshly ground pepper and serve.

Mussel and saffron risotto
This is a really special dish. It may seem involved, but it just requires the stock to be made in advance, and that could be anything from just before you need it to two days ahead of time.

220 g (7¾ oz/1 cup) arborio rice
2 tablespoons unsalted butter, cut into 2 cm
    (¾ inch) cubes
olive oil
½ onion, finely diced
2 garlic cloves, finely chopped
80 ml (2½ fl oz/⅓ cup) dry white wine
2 tablespoons freshly grated Parmesan
sea salt and freshly ground pepper
½ bunch flat-leaf (Italian) parsley, about 75 g
    (2½ oz), roughly chopped

mussel and saffron stock
1 kg (2 lb 4 oz) mussels, scrubbed and de-bearded
80 ml (2½ fl oz/⅓ cup) extra virgin olive oil
1 small red onion, finely diced
1 small leek, finely diced
1 small fennel bulb, finely chopped
4 garlic cloves
sea salt
1.25 litres (44 fl oz/5 cups) chicken stock (page 245)
300 g (10½ oz) white fish fillets, cut into 1 cm
    (½ inch) dice
4 vine-ripened tomatoes, peeled, seeds removed and
    roughly chopped (page 19)
2 bay leaves, fresh if possible
1 small handful parsley and thyme stalks
½ teaspoon saffron threads, simmered for 1 minute
    in 125 ml (4 fl oz/½ cup) water

Serves 4

To make the mussel and saffron stock, put the mussels and 250 ml (9 fl oz/1 cup) water into a saucepan. Place the pan over high heat with a lid on until the mussels begin to open, then remove from the heat. Strain the mussel juice through a fine sieve, reserving the liquid. Check the open mussels for any grit and set aside. Discard any that do not open. Remove the meat from the shells when cool, and discard the shells.

Heat the oil in a large heavy-based saucepan and add the onion, leek, fennel and garlic with a little sea salt. Cook over medium heat until soft but not caramelized. Add the mussel juice, chicken stock, fish, tomato, herbs and saffron and its soaking water and bring to a simmer, skimming off any impurities, for 15 minutes. Remove the pan from the heat and pass through a mouli, food mill or coarse sieve, forcing as much through as possible. Reserve the stock; you will need about 1 litre (35 fl oz/4 cups).

To make the risotto, melt half the butter and a little oil in a large saucepan. Add the onion and garlic and cook slowly until translucent. Add the rice and stir to coat all the grains in the butter, then cook for 30 seconds. Pour in the wine and allow it to reduce completely, then begin adding the stock, ladle by ladle, stirring all the time, and allowing each ladle to be absorbed before you add the next. Continue this for 15–18 minutes until the rice grains are soft but with a firm bite. With the last two ladles of stock, add the reserved mussels. Remove from the heat and add the Parmesan, remaining butter, some salt and pepper and the chopped parsley. Check the seasoning, rest the risotto for 1 minute, then serve straight away in bowls.

Note: Refrigerate or freeze any leftover stock for another use.

Mushroom risotto cakes with zucchini sauce

These great risotto cakes can be prepared in advance, which makes life easy. Any risotto you like can be formed into these cakes; the cakes also make wonderful little canapés when rolled small.

220 g (7³/4 oz/1 cup) arborio rice
10 g (¹/4 oz) dried porcini mushrooms
750 ml (26 fl oz/3 cups) vegetable or chicken stock (page 245)
30 ml (1 fl oz) extra virgin olive oil
1 small onion, finely chopped
2 garlic cloves, finely chopped
sea salt
80 ml (2¹/2 fl oz/¹/3 cup) dry white wine
30 g (1 oz/¹/3 cup) freshly grated Parmesan
1 egg yolk, lightly whisked
140 g (5 oz/2 cups) fresh breadcrumbs
olive oil, for shallow-frying

sautéed mushrooms

250 g (9 oz) field mushrooms, sliced
100 g (3¹/2 oz) Swiss brown mushrooms, sliced
100 g (3¹/2 oz) small button mushrooms, sliced
2 tablespoons unsalted butter, chopped
1 tablespoon extra virgin olive oil
2 garlic cloves, finely chopped
a pinch of chopped thyme
sea salt

zucchini sauce

450 g (1 lb) zucchini (courgette), coarsely grated
1¹/2 tablespoons extra virgin olive oil
4 garlic cloves, finely chopped
3 anchovies, finely chopped
¹/4 teaspoon chilli flakes
80 ml (2¹/2 fl oz/¹/3 cup) water, vegetable or chicken stock (page 245)
1¹/2 tablespoons chopped flat-leaf (Italian) parsley
sea salt and freshly ground pepper

Serves 4

To make the sautéed mushrooms, heat the butter and oil in a large frying pan, then add the garlic, thyme and a pinch of sea salt and cook for 1 minute. Add all the mushrooms and cook, stirring continuously, over high heat for 5–10 minutes, or until the mushrooms release their juices and most of the liquid has evaporated. Remove from the heat and allow to cool.

To make the risotto cakes, soak the porcini mushrooms in 250 ml (9 fl oz/1 cup) boiling water for 20 minutes, or until soft. Drain, reserve the liquid and chop the porcini. Pour the porcini stock into a saucepan with the vegetable or chicken stock and bring to a simmer.

Heat the oil in a large saucepan, add the onion, garlic and a pinch of sea salt and cook over low heat until the onion is soft. Add the rice and stir over medium heat for 2–3 minutes, or until the rice is well coated in the onion mixture and lightly toasted. Add the wine and stir until completely reduced. Add the reserved porcini mushrooms and the stock, ladle by ladle, until the rice is just tender, allowing each ladle to be absorbed before you add the next. Stir in the sautéed mushrooms and Parmesan, mix well and check the seasoning. Remove from the heat and spread over a tray to cool.

When cold, divide the rice into 16 portions and shape each portion into a neat round. Refrigerate for about 30 minutes. Dip the risotto cakes in egg wash and then coat with breadcrumbs. Shallow-fry the cakes in olive oil until crisp and golden. Drain on paper towel.

Meanwhile, to make the zucchini sauce, heat the oil in a small pan over low heat. Add the garlic, anchovies and chilli flakes and cook until the garlic is soft. Increase the heat to medium and add the zucchini. Stir to coat in the oil mixture, then add the water or stock and simmer for several minutes, or until the zucchini is tender. Stir through the parsley and season with salt and pepper to taste.

Spoon the zucchini sauce among four shallow bowls and then arrange the risotto cakes over the top.

Zucchini, basil and chilli risotto This dish can be made as hot as you like. If you like it strong, just add some chilli flakes as well as the fresh chilli. You can make any vegetable risotto this way; just use the cooking liquid as the stock and that takes away the need to make a vegetable stock. If you wish, you can use chicken stock (page 245); it will add a little more body. If you do that, try cooking the vegetables in the chicken stock; again, you are not losing flavour.

220 g (7³/4 oz/1 cup) arborio rice
400 g (14 oz) zucchini (courgette), cut into 5 mm
    (1/4 inch) thick rounds
80 g (2³/4 oz) unsalted butter
extra virgin olive oil
1/2 onion, finely diced
2 garlic cloves, finely chopped
1–2 long red chillies, seeds removed and
    finely chopped
80 ml (2¹/2 fl oz/1/3 cup) dry white wine
2 tablespoons roughly chopped basil
2 tablespoons freshly grated Parmesan, plus extra,
    to serve
sea salt and freshly ground pepper

Serves 4

Put 1.5 litres (52 fl oz/6 cups) salted water and 2 tablespoons of the butter in a large saucepan and bring to the boil. Add the zucchini and cook until soft, then remove and set aside. Strain the cooking liquid and reserve — you will need about 1 litre (35 fl oz/ 4 cups).

In a heavy-based frying pan, melt 1 tablespoon of the butter in a little oil and cook the onion, garlic and chilli over low heat until translucent. Add the rice and stir continuously until it starts to stick. Pour in the wine and allow it to reduce completely, then add ladle after ladle of the hot zucchini cooking liquid, stirring all the time and allowing each ladle to be absorbed before you add the next. Be careful not to drown the rice or allow it to dry out. Repeat this process for 15–18 minutes until the rice grains are soft but with a firm bite.

With the last two ladles of stock, add the zucchini, basil, Parmesan and remaining butter and stir through. Check the seasoning and add a little salt if needed. Rest the risotto for 1 minute. Divide among four large pasta bowls and serve with extra Parmesan and freshly ground pepper.

Tomato and pesto tart This is so simple to make and is great for a quick weekend lunch with a green salad. Of course, you can treat these tarts just like pizza and add any combination you like. Try baking the pastry with tomato sauce and grated fontina cheese, and when it is cooked, place smoked salmon curls and a dollop of sour cream on top, sprinkle with chives and you have the best Mother's Day breakfast ever. Make little ones for canapés … a few of these, a cold beer or two and a good game of footy — what a great way to spend your weekend.

1 sheet frozen puff pastry
80 ml (2^1/$_2$ fl oz/^{1}/$_3$ cup) tomato sauce (see below)
   or tomato passata (puréed tomatoes)
2 small vine-ripened tomatoes, sliced thinly into
   rounds
150 g (5^1/$_2$ oz) fresh buffalo mozzarella, torn
1–2 tablespoons freshly grated Parmesan

tomato sauce (makes about 500 ml/17 fl oz/2 cups)
2 tablespoons extra virgin olive oil
4 garlic cloves, thinly sliced
sea salt
800 g (1 lb 12 oz) tinned diced roma (plum) tomatoes
pinch of caster (superfine) sugar
8 basil leaves, torn

pesto
3 garlic cloves
sea salt
2 tablespoons pine nuts
2 tablespoons freshly grated Parmesan
1 bunch basil, about 120 g (4^1/$_4$ oz), leaves picked
extra virgin olive oil
freshly ground pepper

Serves 4

To make the tomato sauce, heat the oil in a large heavy-based saucepan. Add the garlic and a pinch of salt and cook over low heat for 5 minutes, or until soft. Add the tomatoes, their juices and the sugar. Simmer uncovered for 20 minutes. Stir in the basil leaves and check the seasoning. Preheat the oven to 200°C (400°F/ Gas 6), and place a baking tray in the oven to heat up.

Cut 4 x 12 cm (4^1/$_2$ inch) rounds from the pastry, then return the rounds to the freezer until firm. Remove the pastry from the freezer and, working quickly, spread each with tomato sauce — leaving a border of about 1–2 cm (^{1}/$_4$–^{1}/$_2$ inch) all round — then top with a few overlapping tomato slices, mozzarella and a sprinkle of Parmesan. Place the tarts on the preheated tray and bake in the top one-third of the oven, for 15 minutes, or until the pastry is crisp.

Meanwhile, to make the pesto, pound the garlic and some salt together in a mortar, with a pestle. Add the pine nuts and Parmesan and pound, then add the basil and pound further. Add a little oil and some freshly ground pepper to taste.

Remove the tarts from the oven, let cool slightly, then add a large dollop of pesto in the centre. Serve warm.

Note: It is important to work quickly with pastry to get the best results. Work with chilled or partially frozen pastry and bake it (especially puff) in the middle or top part of the oven at a high temperature, until puffed and golden underneath. We preheated the tray in this recipe as the moisture in the tomato and mozzarella can sometimes prevent the pastry from crisping underneath. Use aluminium trays if you have them, as they are better heat conductors than stainless steel or non-stick ones.

Chicken, pork and prawn paella This is the classic paella. To make a great paella you must create a crust at the bottom of the pan — though that doesn't mean burnt, so make sure you use a pan that fits on the cooking ring you are using, in order to give an even spread of heat. Otherwise, if the flame or hot plate only touches a part of the pan you could be in for tears and a smoky-tasting paella. Also, make sure that, unlike risotto, you don't stir the rice once all the ingredients are in and the cooking process begins. I quite often make a large paella in a pan on a barbecue, which isn't as crazy as it seems; the traditional ones were always made over an open fire, so why not get the barbie going? Oh, and a dollop of garlicky aïoli (page 246) works a treat with this paella.

300 g (10½ oz/1½ cups) short or medium-grain rice
2 tablespoons extra virgin olive oil
1 red capsicum (pepper), seeds removed and thickly sliced
500 g (1 lb 2 oz) boneless, skinless chicken thighs, trimmed and cut into 3 cm (1¼ inch) dice
150 g (5½ oz) chorizo, thickly sliced
150 g (5½ oz) mushrooms, thinly sliced
2 garlic cloves, finely chopped
finely grated zest of 1 lemon
500 g (1 lb 2 oz) ripe tomatoes, roughly chopped
12 raw king prawns (shrimp), peeled and deveined with tails intact
150 g (5½ oz) green beans, trimmed, cut into 3 cm (1¼ inch) lengths
2 teaspoons finely chopped rosemary
2 tablespoons chopped flat-leaf (Italian) parsley
¼ teaspoon saffron threads, dissolved in 3 tablespoons hot water
500 ml (17 fl oz/2 cups) hot chicken stock (page 245)
lemon wedges

Serves 4

Heat the oil in a large, deep frying pan or a paella pan. Add the capsicum and cook over medium heat until soft, then remove from the pan. Add the chicken to the pan and cook for 10 minutes, or until well browned, then remove from the pan. Add the chorizo and cook until golden on all sides, then remove. Add the mushroom, garlic and lemon zest and cook over medium heat for 5 minutes. Stir in the tomato and capsicum and cook for a further 5 minutes until the tomato is soft. Add the prawns, beans, rosemary, parsley, saffron and its soaking water, rice, chicken and chorizo. Stir briefly and add the stock. Do not stir again. Reduce the heat to very low and simmer for 25 minutes. Remove from the heat, cover and allow the paella to steam for a further 10 minutes.

Divide the paella among four bowls and serve with lemon wedges.

Note: Do not use a non-stick pan and do not stir right to the bottom of the pan during the initial cooking stage as the thin crust of crispy rice that forms on the bottom is considered one of the best parts of the paella.

Eggplant parmigiana with tomato sauce and basil oil

This dish has been a favourite on Qantas for a number of years. It is like lasagne for vegetarians. You can make it one day and serve it up to three days later. As a matter of fact, I think it is best on day two or three.

1 kg (2 lb 4 oz) small eggplants (aubergines)
sea salt
extra virgin olive oil, for frying
plain (all-purpose) flour, for dusting
300 g (10½ oz) fresh buffalo or cow's milk mozzarella, cut into 3 mm (⅛ inch) thick slices
3 tablespoons freshly grated Parmesan
1 small handful basil leaves, torn

tomato sauce
800 g (1 lb 12 oz) tinned chopped roma (plum) tomatoes
1½ tablespoons extra virgin olive oil
2 garlic cloves, finely diced
1½ teaspoons caster (superfine) sugar
sea salt and freshly ground pepper

basil oil
2 large handfuls basil leaves
250 ml (9 fl oz/1 cup) extra virgin olive oil

Serves 4

To make the basil oil, blanch the basil leaves in boiling water, drain immediately and refresh in iced water. Drain again and squeeze out the excess water. Blend the basil leaves and oil in a blender until well combined, then pour into a jug and let stand overnight. Pour through a strainer lined with muslin (cheesecloth), allowing the solids to be left behind.

To make the tomato sauce, combine the tomatoes and their juice, the oil, garlic and sugar in a saucepan and season with sea salt and freshly ground pepper. Simmer over medium heat until reduced by half. Adjust the seasoning if necessary.

For the eggplant parmigiana, cut the eggplant into 1 cm (½ inch) thick slices lengthways. Place the slices into a colander, sprinkle with salt and let stand for 1 hour. Rinse the eggplant to remove the salt and pat dry with paper towel.

Heat a shallow layer of oil in a frying pan, dust the eggplant slices in flour and shake off any excess. Shallow-fry the eggplant, in batches, until golden brown on both sides, then drain on paper towel.

To assemble, lightly grease a 2.25 litre (79 fl oz/9 cup) baking dish and line the base with a layer of fried eggplant. Spread with some tomato sauce, then scatter with a little of the mozzarella, Parmesan and basil leaves. Repeat this process twice, then finish with a final layer of eggplant. Bake the parmigiana in a preheated oven at 180°C (350°F/Gas 4) for 10–15 minutes, or until warmed through. Divide the parmigiana among four plates and serve with basil oil.

Baked zucchini with goat's cheese 'lasagne'

Vegetarian food is very important on Qantas, and we include one dish on every menu. It has also become a very important offering at Rockpool: we have the vegetarian tasting menu, and a vegetarian dish in each course. This dish can easily be changed, to give you more variety. Try it with eggplant (aubergine) instead of zucchini, or even strips of capsicum (pepper), and the goat's cheese can be changed to ricotta, again, to change texture and flavour.

4 large zucchini (courgettes), cut into 5 mm (¼ inch) thick slices on the diagonal
olive oil
200 g (7 oz) soft goat's cheese

breadcrumb filling
3 tablespoons extra virgin olive oil
1 small red onion, finely chopped
100 g (3½ oz/1½ cups) sourdough breadcrumbs
50 g (1¾ oz/⅓ cup) pitted green olives, finely chopped
50 g (1¾ oz/⅓ cup) pitted kalamata olives, finely chopped
40 g (1½ oz/¼ cup) pine nuts, roasted
2 tablespoons dried currants
1 tablespoon salted capers, rinsed

tomato sauce
2 tablespoons extra virgin olive oil
3 garlic cloves, thinly sliced
sea salt and freshly ground pepper
1 small fresh red chilli, finely chopped
3 tablespoons dry white wine
800 g (1 lb 12 oz) tinned whole roma (plum) tomatoes, roughly chopped
½ teaspoon caster (superfine) sugar
1 tablespoon finely chopped basil

Serves 4

Toss the zucchini with oil, and then cook in a large frying pan over high heat until golden on both sides.

To make the breadcrumb filling, heat the oil in a large frying pan and cook the onion over low heat for about 8 minutes, or until soft. Add the breadcrumbs and cook until golden. Remove from the heat and stir in the remaining ingredients.

To make the tomato sauce, heat the oil in a large frying pan over low–medium heat. Add the garlic, salt and pepper and cook over low heat for about 5 minutes, or until the garlic is starting to colour. Add the chilli and cook for a further minute. Add the wine and simmer until reduced, then stir in the chopped tomato, sugar and basil. Simmer, uncovered, for about 20 minutes, or until the sauce has reduced and thickened. Check the seasoning and adjust if necessary.

Preheat the oven to 200°C (400°F/Gas 6). To assemble, line the base of four 350 ml (12 fl oz) ramekins with half the zucchini slices, overlapping them if necessary. Spoon half of the tomato sauce over the zucchini and then sprinkle over half of the crumbs, then half of the goat's cheese. Repeat layering with the remaining zucchini, sauce, crumbs and goat's cheese. Drizzle the top of each with a little extra olive oil before baking for 5–10 minutes, or until the cheese is golden. Cool slightly before serving.

Mussels with walnut tarator I love this sauce — it is easy to make and can be made with a combination of nuts, or a single variety. Try having it with barbecued or roast chicken, and it is also lovely tossed with some freshly sautéed squid or prawns (shrimp). It will definitely stay in the repertoire if you make it once.

2 kg (4 lb 8 oz) mussels, scrubbed and de-bearded
3 tablespoons dry white wine
extra virgin olive oil
1 handful flat-leaf (Italian) parsley leaves, chopped

tarator
50 g (1¾ oz/1½ cup) walnuts, roasted
80 g (2¾ oz/½ cup) pine nuts
2 garlic cloves, crushed
sea salt
80 g (2¾ oz/1 cup) fresh breadcrumbs
freshly ground pepper
juice of 2 small lemons
250 ml (9 fl oz/1 cup) extra virgin olive oil

Serves 4

In a mortar with a pestle, make the tarator by pounding the walnuts, pine nuts, garlic and some sea salt to a paste. Add the breadcrumbs and a dash of water and pound to mix through. Add ground pepper and lemon juice, then slowly add the oil, a little at a time, and pound to a creamy consistency. Check the seasoning.

Add the white wine to a large saucepan, cover with a tight-fitting lid and place over high heat. When steaming, quickly remove the lid, add the mussels and replace the lid. Steam until the mussels just pop open. Transfer the mussels and juices to a mixing bowl and discard any mussels that have not opened. Add the tarator, a dash of oil and the parsley to the mussels and mix to combine. Divide among four plates and serve.

Steamed mussels with spicy broth I love the simplicity of this dish. The butter at the end enriches the sauce, but if you don't like it by all means just leave it out, it will still be yum. To give the dish more substance, add some cooked pasta just before serving. I also love to serve a dollop of freshly-made aïoli (page 246) on this dish, as the more garlic the merrier when it comes to mussels.

1.5 kg (3 lb 5 oz) mussels, scrubbed and de-bearded
extra virgin olive oil
1 red onion, sliced
4 garlic cloves, sliced
1 teaspoon chilli flakes
2 tablespoons salted baby capers, rinsed
1/2 bunch flat-leaf (Italian) parsley, about 75 g (2 1/2 oz), roughly chopped
150 ml (5 fl oz) dry white wine
3 tablespoons unsalted butter
freshly ground pepper
juice of 1 lemon

Serves 4

Heat a little oil in a large saucepan with a tight-fitting lid. Add the onion, garlic and chilli flakes and sauté for about 5 minutes. Add the mussels, capers, parsley and wine, then cover and cook until the mussels open, discarding any that don't. Add the butter and stir to combine with the pepper and lemon juice. Check the seasoning and serve with toasted bread.

Sautéed squid with chilli and radicchio This is just delicious. I love radicchio in anything, but when it's warm, I'm really mad for it. What makes this a superb dish, besides the fact that fresh squid and radicchio are great, are the fried breadcrumbs; they add a wonderful crunch and a caramelized flavour. The dish is also very pretty.

800 g (1 lb 12 oz) cleaned squid tubes, opened up and cut into strips
extra virgin olive oil
1 red onion, finely diced
4 garlic cloves, finely chopped
4 anchovies, roughly chopped
4 small red chillies, seeds removed and finely diced
sea salt
1 radicchio, leaves washed and shredded
4 vine-ripened tomatoes, peeled, seeds removed and roughly chopped (page 19)
1 handful flat-leaf (Italian) parsley leaves, chopped
1 tablespoon salted baby capers, rinsed
splash of balsamic vinegar
80 g (2³⁄₄ oz/1 cup) fresh breadcrumbs
freshly ground pepper
juice of 1 lemon

Serves 2

Heat some oil in a frying pan over high heat. Add the onion, garlic, anchovies, chilli and some sea salt and cook for 2 minutes, stirring. Add the squid and toss for 1 minute. Add the radicchio, tomato, parsley, capers, balsamic vinegar and a little more sea salt and cook for a further 1 minute to warm everything through. Check the seasoning, then tip the contents of the pan onto a large plate.

Wipe out the pan and add a little more oil. When hot, add the breadcrumbs, season with sea salt and freshly ground pepper and fry until crisp. Spoon the crisp crumbs over the squid, squeeze over the lemon juice and serve.

Sautéed king prawns with tomato and avocado salsa This salsa goes well with any seafood. You can cut the vegetable dice as fine or chunky as you like, depending on how delicate or rustic you want the dish to be. Lime juice would be a welcome substitute for lemon, and I often add a couple of really hot wild green chillies, but then I'm just addicted to chillies.

16 large green king prawns (shrimp), peeled and
    deveined
extra virgin olive oil
sea salt and freshly ground pepper

tomato and avocado salsa
4 small vine-ripened tomatoes, roughly diced
1/2 large avocado, stone removed, roughly diced
1/2 red onion, roughly diced
6 basil leaves, torn
extra virgin olive oil
sea salt and freshly ground pepper
juice of 2 lemons

Serves 4

Heat a little oil in a large frying pan. Add the prawns and cook for 2 minutes. Turn over and cook for a further 2 minutes, or until done. Remove to a bowl and season the prawns with sea salt, freshly ground pepper and a dash of oil.

To make the salsa, mix the tomato, avocado, onion and basil. Add a splash of oil and season with salt and pepper to taste and the juice of 1 lemon.

Arrange the salsa in the middle of four large plates, top with four prawns for each plate and squeeze the remaining lemon juice over, then serve.

Barbecued king prawns, split and marinated

Like the salsa for the previous recipe, this marinade can be used to marinate any seafood. If you feel like spoiling your friends, split a lobster in half for every two people, marinate and barbecue, taking care not to overcook it. You need really large prawns (shrimp) for this dish so you can pull the flesh out easily once they are cooked. Another way to cook these prawns is to lay them out on a tray and place them under the grill (broiler) element of the oven; they really come out wonderfully delicious that way and if the weather's not great, you don't have to venture out to the barbecue.

16 extra large green king prawns (shrimp), shell on,
    cut lengthways down the middle
extra virgin olive oil
juice of 1 lemon
freshly ground pepper

marinade
grated zest of 1 lemon
3 garlic cloves, peeled
2 cm (3/4 inch) piece ginger, peeled and grated
1 teaspoon chilli flakes
1 tablespoon chopped oregano
1 tablespoon chopped sage
1 tablespoon chopped coriander (cilantro) leaves
sea salt
100 ml (3 1/2 fl oz) extra virgin olive oil, plus extra,
    to serve

Serves 4

To make the marinade, place all the ingredients except the oil in a mortar and crush with a pestle to a coarse paste. Mix in the oil. Place the prawns in a large bowl and pour over the marinade. Allow to stand for 1 hour at room temperature.

Preheat the barbecue, making sure the bars are clean. Place the prawns on the barbecue for 1 minute, then turn over. After another minute, remove from the barbecue and divide among four large plates. Drizzle with oil and fresh lemon juice and give a generous grind of fresh pepper.

Dry curry of prawns This southern Indian-style curry is great with any seafood. Try stir-frying some scallops, or squid, or even a combination of these and prawns. You can also add 250 ml (9 fl oz/1 cup) coconut milk to the curry to make more gravy for your rice; it will taste quite different, but delicious all the same.

16 large green king prawns (shrimp), peeled and deveined
4 vine-ripened tomatoes
vegetable oil
3 cm (1¼ inch) piece ginger, peeled and roughly chopped
6 garlic cloves, roughly chopped
2 teaspoons black mustard seeds
2 dried long red chillies, seeds removed and roughly chopped
¼ teaspoon ground turmeric
1½ teaspoons sea salt
¼ teaspoon freshly ground pepper
8 snake (yard-long) beans, cut into 3 cm (1¼ inch) lengths
juice of 2 limes

Serves 4

Preheat the oven to 150°C (300°F/Gas 2). Place the tomatoes on a baking tray and drizzle with a little oil. Slow roast the tomatoes for 1½ hours, or until they are soft. Allow them to cool slightly before removing and discarding the skin and mashing the flesh.

Pound the ginger and garlic in a mortar with a pestle to form a rough paste. Remove and set aside.

Crush the mustard seeds with the chilli in the mortar, then add the turmeric, sea salt and freshly ground pepper, mix and set aside.

Heat some oil in a heavy-based frying pan and cook the ginger and garlic paste until lightly coloured and caramelized. Add the prepared spices and stir over low heat until fragrant. Stir through the tomato flesh and simmer the sauce for several minutes to reduce slightly. Set aside.

Heat a large wok or pan with a little oil and stir-fry the prawns over high heat until cooked. You will need to do this in two batches. Remove the prawns and set them aside in a bowl. Add the snake beans to the wok and stir-fry to heat through. Return the prawns and tomato curry to the wok. Mix together well. Finish with the lime juice to taste.

Divide the prawn curry among four large bowls and serve with rice.

Stir-fried king prawns with black beans and ginger The simplest of stir-fries … you can use any vegetable you like instead of the snow peas, or a combination. The art of stir-frying is to have a very hot wok or pan and to work quickly. You want to cook the ingredients quickly, at high heat, so you may have to cook the stir-fry in batches. This way, the ingredients are stir-fried, not stewed, and the wok retains its heat throughout the cooking process.

16 large green king prawns (shrimp), peeled and deveined
80 ml (2^{1}/$_{2}$ fl oz/^{1}/$_{3}$ cup) vegetable oil
100 g (3^{1}/$_{2}$ oz/1 cup) snow peas (mangetout), trimmed
2 tablespoons fermented black beans
2 garlic cloves, finely chopped
3 cm (1^{1}/$_{4}$ inch) piece ginger, peeled and cut into julienne
^{1}/$_{2}$ red capsicum (pepper), seeds removed and finely chopped
^{1}/$_{2}$ green capsicum (pepper), seeds removed and finely chopped
4 spring onions (scallions), cut into 3 cm (1^{1}/$_{4}$ inch) lengths
2 tablespoons shaoxing rice wine
2 tablespoons light soy sauce
1 tablespoon oyster sauce
2 teaspoons caster (superfine) sugar
125 ml (4 fl oz/^{1}/$_{2}$ cup) chicken stock (page 245)
1 small handful coriander (cilantro) leaves
1 spring onion (scallion), cut into julienne

Serves 4

Heat half the oil in a wok until just smoking. Stir-fry half the prawns until they change colour and are almost cooked through, then remove from the wok and place in a bowl. Repeat the process with the remaining prawns and place into the bowl. Cook the snow peas in two batches as well, about 1 minute per batch.

If necessary, add more oil to the wok and stir-fry the black beans, garlic, ginger, red and green capsicum and spring onion until fragrant. De-glaze with the shaoxing wine, then add the soy and oyster sauces, sugar and stock. Reduce the sauce until it thickens, then return the prawns and snow peas to the wok. Check the seasoning, add the coriander and toss to combine. Divide among four large bowls. Top with julienne of spring onion and serve with rice.

Barbecued tuna with orange and olive salad

As long as you don't overcook the tuna you will love this dish. Like the sauces and salsas in this book, the salad lends itself to other fish and meat cooked a variety of ways. Barbecuing introduces a nice smokiness to the taste.

4 x 185 g (6½ oz) tuna steaks
sea salt
extra virgin olive oil
freshly ground pepper

orange and olive salad
120 g (4¼ oz) green olives, pitted and halved
2 French shallots, thinly sliced
4 red radishes, cut into thin rounds
4 oranges, segmented (page 83)
1 handful mint leaves
2 spring onions (scallions), cut into thin rounds

dressing
100 ml (3½ fl oz) extra virgin olive oil
juice of 1 orange
juice of 1 lime
2 tablespoons red wine vinegar
2 teaspoons grated palm sugar (jaggery)
zest of ½ orange
sea salt and freshly ground pepper

Serves 4

To make the dressing, whisk together all the ingredients and check the seasoning.

Sprinkle the tuna steaks with a little sea salt and drizzle with a little oil. Heat the barbecue grill to hot and cook the tuna steaks for 2 minutes. Turn over and cook for a further 2 minutes, being careful not to overcook the tuna. Allow to rest in a warm place for 2 minutes.

Combine the salad ingredients in a bowl and toss with the dressing. Serve the tuna on large plates and place the salad on top of the fish. Give a good grind of fresh pepper and serve.

Great with: Roast potatoes (page 242), aïoli (page 246) and boiled asparagus.

Seared tuna with romesco sauce

Romesco sauce is one of the classic Spanish salsas. It does have a few ingredients, but it is so simple to make that, once you do, you will be eating it with everything and making it over and over again. Trust me, it is so addictive. The sauce will keep in the fridge for about a week, so don't worry that it is more than enough for four people.

4 x 185 g (6½ oz) tuna steaks
extra virgin olive oil
sea salt and freshly ground pepper
1 lemon

romesco sauce
160 ml (5¼ fl oz) extra virgin olive oil
4 small red chillies, split and seeds removed
4 garlic cloves, halved lengthways
1 slice Italian-style bread, about 50 g (1¾ oz), crusts removed and roughly chopped
40 g (1½ oz/¼ cup) blanched almonds
35 g (1¼ oz/¼ cup) skinned hazelnuts, roasted
2 red capsicums (peppers), roasted, peeled and chopped (page 176) or 250 g (9 oz) prepared roasted red capsicum, chopped
2 vine-ripened tomatoes, peeled, seeds removed and chopped (page 19)
1 tablespoon sherry vinegar
1 small handful flat-leaf (Italian) parsley leaves, chopped
sea salt and freshly ground pepper

Serves 4

To make the romesco sauce, heat 3 tablespoons of the oil in a small frying pan, then add the chilli, garlic, bread and almonds and cook over medium heat for 2–3 minutes, or until the bread and almonds are golden. Cool slightly, then process the bread mixture with the hazelnuts, capsicum and tomato until well combined. With the motor running, add the remaining oil in a thin, steady stream until the sauce is smooth but still slightly textured. Stir in the sherry vinegar and parsley and adjust the seasoning as necessary.

Drizzle the tuna with a little oil and sprinkle with sea salt on both sides. Heat a large pan until hot and just smoking. Add the tuna to the pan and cook for about 2 minutes, depending on the thickness, until a good crust forms. Turn and cook for a further minute, then remove and rest in a warm place for 1 minute. Place a piece of fish on each plate and top with some romesco, a sprinkle of sea salt and freshly ground pepper and a squeeze of fresh lemon — I like to add a drizzle of oil as well — then serve.

Great with: Steamed green beans.

Seared salmon with cucumber and mint salsa The two vinegars in this salsa work well together — they add complexity of taste — but by all means just use one or the other if you wish, or even omit both and use lemon juice. Another nice variation is to replace the horseradish relish with wholegrain dijon mustard.

4 x 185 g (6¹/2 oz) pieces salmon fillet, skin on
sea salt
extra virgin olive oil

cucumber and mint salsa
1 handful mint leaves, roughly chopped
2 small French shallots, roughly chopped
¹/2 Lebanese (short) cucumber, seeds removed and
    thinly sliced
sea salt
2 teaspoons red wine vinegar
2 teaspoons balsamic vinegar
1 tablespoon good-quality horseradish relish
100 ml (3¹/2 fl oz) extra virgin olive oil
2 teaspoons caster (superfine) sugar
2 spring onions (scallions), white part only, cut
    into rounds
freshly ground pepper

Serves 4

To make the salsa, place the mint, French shallots and cucumber in a bowl with a pinch of sea salt. Add the vinegars, horseradish, oil, sugar and spring onion. Give a generous grind of fresh pepper and check the seasoning. Mix well and leave for 15 minutes.

Scrape the skin of the salmon with the back of a knife, moving backwards and forwards to remove most of the moisture, then season with sea salt and drizzle with a little oil.

Place the fish into a hot frying pan, skin side down. Cook for about 3 minutes on the first side, turn over and cook a further 2 minutes on the other side. Allow to rest for a couple of minutes. The salmon should be medium rare. If you like it cooked more, just give it more time, but you may want to lower the heat so it doesn't burn. Place a salmon steak on each plate and top with the cucumber and mint salsa.

Great with: Potato gratin (page 241) and steamed green beans.

Crispy skin salmon with braised chickpeas and herbed yoghurt Use a tin of cooked chickpeas here to really speed the recipe up. The salmon skin is made crisp by first removing any water trapped in the skin and then cooking it for the longest time skin side down, and then giving it a quick turn and just a little sear on the other side.

4 x 185 g (6¹/₂ oz) pieces salmon fillet, skin on
sea salt
extra virgin olive oil
1 lemon
freshly ground pepper

braised chickpeas
400 g (14 oz) dried chickpeas, or 700 g (1 lb 9 oz) tinned
    cooked chickpeas
2 tablespoons extra virgin olive oil
2 garlic cloves, thinly sliced
8 sage leaves
400 g (14 oz) tinned whole roma (plum) tomatoes,
    juice reserved, roughly chopped
sea salt and freshly ground pepper

herbed yoghurt
2 tablespoons chopped coriander (cilantro) leaves
2 tablespoons chopped mint
juice of ¹/₂ lemon
125 g (4¹/₂ oz/1 cup) sheep's milk yoghurt
sea salt and freshly ground pepper

Serves 4

To make the braised chickpeas, soak the dried chickpeas in cold water for 24 hours, or bring to the boil in water, then drain and refresh. Place the chickpeas in a heavy-based saucepan, cover with fresh water and bring to the boil. Skim and simmer gently for about 30 minutes, or until tender, then drain.

Heat the oil in a heavy-based pan, fry the garlic and sage for about 1 minute, then add the chickpeas, tomatoes and their juice, salt and pepper. Simmer gently for about 15 minutes. Check the seasoning.

To make the herbed yoghurt, add all the ingredients to a bowl and mix. Season well.

Scrape the skin of the salmon with the back of a knife moving backwards and forwards to remove most of the moisture, then season with sea salt and drizzle with oil. Heat a frying pan until smoking hot, add the salmon, skin side down, and cook for about 3 minutes, or until the skin is crisp and the fish is cooked about one-third of the way through. Turn the fish and cook for a further minute or two. Remove from the pan and rest for 1 minute in a warm place.

Divide the braised chickpeas among four large plates and place the salmon on top, skin side up. Add a dollop of herbed yoghurt, a squeeze of lemon juice, a sprinkle of sea salt and a grind of pepper.

Pan-fried marinated salmon with cucumber and radish relish

This is a beautiful little salad to add to the top of the fish; it is very pretty and fresh tasting. If you don't have time to marinate the fish, don't worry, try that next time, it will still taste great. Don't forget to concentrate on not overcooking the fish.

4 x 185 g (6$^{1}/_{2}$ oz) pieces salmon fillet, skin removed

marinade
100 ml (3$^{1}/_{2}$ fl oz) extra virgin olive oil
3 small red chillies, seeds removed and finely diced
1 teaspoon ground cumin
1 teaspoon ground coriander
1 teaspoon paprika
1 teaspoon ground turmeric
grated zest of $^{1}/_{2}$ lemon
juice of 1 lemon
2 tablespoons chopped coriander (cilantro) leaves
sea salt

radish relish
8 red radishes
3 Lebanese (short) cucumbers, peeled, halved
    and seeds removed
1 celery stalk
100 ml (3$^{1}/_{2}$ fl oz) extra virgin olive oil
2 tablespoons red wine vinegar
1 teaspoon wholegrain mustard
sea salt and freshly ground pepper
1 large handful mint leaves

Serves 4

To make the marinade, process all the ingredients together (it is not important for it to be completely puréed). Marinate the fish fillets in the marinade for 2 hours.

Meanwhile, make the relish. Using a Japanese mandolin, slice the radishes, cucumber and celery very finely (otherwise, if your knife work is good, by all means just use a very sharp knife). Whisk the oil, vinegar and mustard together in a bowl, and then season with sea salt and freshly ground pepper to taste. Add the prepared vegetables and mint leaves to the dressing and mix to combine.

Heat a frying pan, grill (broiler) or barbecue to hot. Remove the fish from the marinade and place it over the heat, presentation side down. Cook for 2 minutes and turn, cook for a further minute, or until almost cooked through, then rest in a warm place for about 1 minute. Place a piece of fish on each plate and top with the relish.

Pan-fried ocean trout with creamed lentils
This dish can be made even more simple by having a tin of cooked lentils in the cupboard, which is nothing to be ashamed of; sometimes speed is of the essence.

4 x 185 g (6 1/2 oz) pieces ocean trout fillet, skin on
extra virgin olive oil
sea salt and freshly ground pepper
1 lemon

creamed lentils
150 g (5 1/2 oz/3/4 cup) puy lentils or tiny blue-green
   lentils
extra virgin olive oil
1 tablespoon unsalted butter
1 slice smoky bacon, diced
1/2 small onion, finely diced
1 garlic clove
1 small carrot, finely diced
2 thyme sprigs
sea salt
400 ml (14 fl oz) chicken stock (page 245)
1 tablespoon shredded basil
1/4 bunch chives, about 5 g (1/8 oz), chopped
juice of 1/2 lemon
125 ml (4 fl oz/1/2 cup) cream (whipping)

Serves 4

To make the creamed lentils, add the lentils to a saucepan of cold water and bring to the boil. Drain the lentils and rinse well under cold water.

Add a little oil and the butter to a deep frying pan and, when foaming, add the bacon, onion, garlic, carrot and thyme, and cook until the vegetables are soft, but not brown. Add the lentils, sea salt and enough stock to just cover. Bring to the boil, reduce the heat immediately and simmer slowly for about 25 minutes, or until the lentils are just tender, and most of the liquid has evaporated. Stir through the basil, chives, lemon juice and cream. Process 170 ml (5 1/2 fl oz/2/3 cup) of the lentil mixture until smooth. Return the purée to the lentil mixture and stir to combine. Check the seasoning.

Drizzle the ocean trout with a little oil and sprinkle with sea salt. Heat a frying pan until just smoking and place the fish in, skin side down. Cook for 3 minutes, or until the skin is crisp and then turn, cook for a further minute, remove, and rest in a warm place for 1 minute.

Spoon a portion of lentils onto each plate and place the fish on top, skin side up. Drizzle with extra oil, sprinkle with sea salt, give a grind of pepper and a little squeeze of lemon juice and serve.

Roast barramundi with cauliflower, fennel seeds and breadcrumbs

If you love cauliflower as much as I do, you will make this dish often. It can be adapted to use other seafood and roasted meats.

4 x 185 g (6½ oz) pieces barramundi fillet, or other firm white fish fillet
1 small cauliflower, cut into florets
extra virgin olive oil
2 garlic cloves, thinly sliced
1 dried long red chilli, crushed
2 teaspoons fennel seeds
300 g (10½ oz) cherry tomatoes, halved and seeds squeezed out
sea salt and freshly ground pepper
1 small handful basil leaves
50 g (1¾ oz/½ cup) coarse sourdough breadcrumbs, toasted
juice of 1 lemon

Serves 4

Cut the cauliflower florets into half lengthways. Heat the oil in a heavy-based pan and add the garlic, chilli and fennel seeds. Cook until the garlic has slightly coloured, then add the cauliflower and cook until lightly browned. Add the tomato, season to taste and cook gently for 10–15 minutes.

While the cauliflower mixture is cooking, preheat the oven to 180°C (350°F/Gas 4). Heat an ovenproof pan with a little oil. Season the barramundi lightly with sea salt and cook on one side until golden, then turn over and place in the oven to roast for about 5 minutes. Remove the fish from the oven when it is just cooked.

Add the basil and breadcrumbs to the cauliflower mixture and stir though. Place a large spoonful of the cauliflower mixture on each plate and top with the barramundi, then drizzle with oil, lemon juice and freshly ground pepper.

Great with: Potato purée (page 243) and boiled peas.

Roast barramundi with garam masala marinade
Use any fish for this dish. You can add a crushed garlic clove to the yoghurt to really add flavour, and a couple of chillies to the marinade will certainly kick it on.

4 x 185 g (6½ oz) pieces barramundi fillet, or other firm white fish fillet
extra virgin olive oil
125 g (4½ oz/½ cup) sheep's milk yoghurt, seasoned with lemon juice, sea salt and freshly ground pepper
1 lemon, cut into wedges

marinade
4 garlic cloves, finely chopped
1 small red onion, chopped
1 tablespoon chopped flat-leaf (Italian) parsley
1 tablespoon chopped coriander (cilantro) leaves
1 tablespoon garam masala
100 ml (3½ fl oz) extra virgin olive oil
sea salt

Serves 4

To make the marinade, combine all the ingredients and blend until well combined. Cover the barramundi with the marinade and allow to sit for about 1 hour at room temperature.

Preheat the oven to 180°C (350°F/Gas 4). Heat some oil in a heavy-based, ovenproof frying pan. Sear the barramundi fillets on both sides, then transfer the pan to the oven for 5 minutes, or until the fish fillets are just cooked through.

Place a barramundi fillet on each plate, dollop the yoghurt on the side and season the fillets with a little sea salt and freshly ground pepper. Serve a lemon wedge on each plate.

Great with: Potato purée (page 243) and steamed asparagus dressed with a little extra virgin olive oil and lemon juice.

Barbecued swordfish with roast tomato and balsamic vinegar sauce You don't need to create the grill marks; it adds nothing to the taste, but the look is real restaurant stuff and if the grill bars are clean, very easy to do. Use tuna or any other fish you like instead of the swordfish. This sauce is a cracker with roast chicken or barbecued lamb cutlets as well.

4 x 185 g (6$^1/_2$ oz) swordfish steaks
extra virgin olive oil
sea salt
juice of 1 lemon
freshly ground pepper

roast tomato sauce
5 vine-ripened tomatoes, cores removed
80 ml (2$^1/_2$ fl oz/$^1/_3$ cup) extra virgin olive oil
50 ml (1$^1/_2$ fl oz) balsamic vinegar
$^1/_4$ bunch tarragon, about 5 g ($^1/_8$ oz), finely chopped
$^1/_4$ bunch thyme, about 5 g ($^1/_8$ oz), finely chopped
caster (superfine) sugar
sea salt and freshly ground pepper

Serves 4

To make the roast tomato sauce, preheat the oven to 150°C (300°F/Gas 2). Put the tomatoes on a baking tray and sprinkle with the oil, balsamic vinegar, herbs, a little sugar and seasoning. Roast for 30–40 minutes, or until the skins start to blister and peel. Remove the tomato skins with a pair of tongs and discard. Pass the tomato through a food mill with the herbs and any residual liquid. Put the sauce into a saucepan and reduce for 30 minutes over very low heat. Check the seasoning. If the tomato sauce is a little tart, add a pinch of sugar and more salt.

Preheat the barbecue. Rub the swordfish with oil and sprinkle with sea salt. Place the steaks at a 45-degree angle to the straight bars and cook for 1 minute, then rotate the steaks 45 degrees the other way for 1 minute. Turn the steaks over and cook for a further 1$^1/_2$ minutes before removing from the heat. Rest the fish in a warm place for a few minutes.

To serve, place a generous spoonful of tomato sauce on each plate, place the fish on top, drizzle with oil and lemon juice and season with freshly ground pepper.

Great with: Potato salad (page 241) and steamed spinach with extra virgin olive oil.

Barbecued Hiramasa kingfish with chilli and herb marinade and aïoli

I love the flavour of barbecued seafood paired with the garlicky taste of aïoli. This would be perfect with a potato salad and some barbecued asparagus. What a great lunch.

4 x 185 g (6½ oz) pieces Hiramasa kingfish fillet
1 lemon, cut into wedges
4 tablespoons aïoli (page 246)
freshly ground pepper

marinade
2 garlic cloves
2 fresh long red chillies, seeds removed
zest of ½ lemon
1 handful flat-leaf (Italian) parsley leaves
3 tablespoons oregano leaves
sea salt and freshly ground pepper
extra virgin olive oil

Serves 4

To make the marinade, simply blend all the ingredients, except the oil, together until smooth, or pound the ingredients in a mortar with a pestle. Gradually incorporate just enough oil to loosen the mixture. Season to taste, coat the fillets in the marinade and set aside for about 1 hour at room temperature.

Heat the barbecue to medium and grill the fish until medium–rare, turning just once; they will need about 2 minutes on each side. Don't have the barbecue searing hot, or the marinade will burn.

Place each kingfish fillet on a large plate, serve with a lemon wedge, a dollop of aïoli on top and a good grind of fresh pepper.

Whiting, Sicilian-style The sweet-sour nature of this beautiful dish comes from the two-century Moorish occupation of Sicily. Lots of Sicilian cooking involves fruit, and couscous is used often. Serve any of the delicious leftover sauce with pan-fried chicken, duck or lamb. It is not always necessary to pin-bone fish before cooking, but it does make for easier eating. Simply take a pair of fish tweezers (available from kitchenware shops), feel for the bones with your fingers, gently press down on the flesh either side of the bone and pluck the bones out — it is that easy. This meal looks great as a banquet-style dish — serve it on a large platter with the couscous on the side.

8 large whiting fillets, pin-boned
extra virgin olive oil
1 red onion, diced
sea salt
2 celery stalks, diced
50 g (1¾ oz/⅓ cup) pine nuts, roasted
50 g (1¾ oz/⅓ cup) currants or raisins
2 tablespoons honey
3 tablespoons red wine vinegar
1 handful dill, roughly chopped
½ bunch chives, about 15 g (½ oz), roughly chopped
freshly ground pepper

Serves 4

Heat a little oil in a large pan. Place the fish in the pan, skin side down. Cook for about 1 minute, then gently turn over and cook for about 30 seconds on the other side. You will need to cook the fish in two or three batches. Remove the fillets and place on a baking tray, keeping them warm in the oven while you cook the others. Be careful not to overcook the fish as it has a very delicate flesh.

Heat a little more oil in a separate pan and add the onion and some sea salt. Cook until softened. Add the celery, a dash more oil, the pine nuts and the currants or raisins, then the honey, red wine vinegar, dill and chives. Grind on some fresh pepper. You should have a sweet-sour tasting vinaigrette. Place two fish fillets on each plate and spoon a generous amount of the sauce over the top. Alternatively, serve this dish banquet-style, on a large platter with couscous on the side.

Great with: Couscous (page 244), salad and some steamed snow peas (mangetout).

Whole barbecued King George whiting with tomato and onion sauce

The extra flavour from cooking the sauce on the barbecue is wonderful and easy to do. Try any whole fish you like here. Scoring the fish does two things — it helps to cook it evenly and gives you a look inside, so you can tell when it is cooked.

4 whole King George whiting, about 500 g (1 lb 2 oz) each, scored both sides to the bone
sea salt
extra virgin olive oil

tomato and onion sauce
4 large vine-ripened tomatoes, sliced 5 mm (1/4 inch) thick
sea salt
extra virgin olive oil
1 large red onion, sliced
balsamic vinegar
freshly ground pepper

salad
1 handful mint leaves
1 handful coriander (cilantro) leaves
1 handful flat-leaf (Italian) parsley leaves
1 tablespoon oregano leaves
verjuice
extra virgin olive oil
sea salt and freshly ground pepper

Serves 4

First make the sauce. Season the tomato slices with sea salt, drizzle with a little oil and place them on the flat plate of a medium–hot barbecue. Add the onion to the tomato, season with salt and turn the mixture regularly. When the sauce is nicely coloured and soft, place it into a bowl and leave for 5 minutes. Add some extra oil and salt, a splash of balsamic vinegar and lots of freshly ground pepper and mash with a fork.

Meanwhile, season the whole fish with salt, drizzle with oil and cook on a hot part of the barbecue for about 5 minutes. Carefully turn the fish over, drizzle with a little more oil and sprinkle with a little more sea salt and continue cooking until just cooked through. Transfer the fish to four large plates and spoon the sauce beside the fish.

Mix the herbs together with a splash of verjuice, oil, salt and pepper. Mix well and sprinkle over the fish.

Great with: Salad and potato chips (page 242).

Herb-crusted snapper and crunchy salsa

This is a great way to cook fish. At Qantas catering, we use crusts of all kinds, as they help protect the fish from the heat of the oven and keep it moist. So add any herbs and spices you like to create your own topping for the fish.

4 x 185 g (6½ oz) pieces snapper fillet, skin removed

coriander crust
50 g (1¾ oz/½ cup) sourdough breadcrumbs
2 large handfuls coriander (cilantro) leaves
1 tablespoon pine nuts, roasted
2 tablespoons freshly grated Parmesan
30 ml (1 fl oz) olive oil
sea salt

crunchy salsa
1 long green chilli, seeds removed and finely chopped
1 small red capsicum (pepper), seeds removed and finely diced
1 small green capsicum (pepper), seeds removed and finely diced
2 garlic cloves, finely chopped
3 spring onions (scallions), thinly sliced on the diagonal
1 small Lebanese (short) cucumber, peeled, seeds removed and finely diced
4 roma (plum) tomatoes, quartered, seeds removed and finely diced
1 small handful coriander (cilantro) leaves, roughly chopped
80 ml (2½ fl oz/⅓ cup) extra virgin olive oil
juice of 2 limes
sea salt and freshly ground pepper

Serves 4

To make the coriander crust, place the breadcrumbs, coriander, pine nuts and Parmesan in a food processor and process until well combined. With the motor running, add the oil in a continuous stream. Season with sea salt.

To make the salsa, combine all the ingredients in a large bowl and season to taste. Preheat the oven to 200°C (400°F/Gas 6).

Spread a thin layer of the coriander crust over one side of the snapper fillets, then place, crust side up, in a roasting dish. Pour a film of water into the dish (this helps keep the fish moist, and it will evaporate during the cooking process). Roast the snapper in the hot oven for 8–10 minutes, or until the fish is slightly opaque under the crust. Serve the fish with a large spoonful of salsa on the side.

Great with: Parsnip purée and steamed broccoli.

Barbecued snapper with green olive and tomato sauce I love this sauce with the green olives, as they have a wonderful nuttiness; however, it is also delicious with black ones, just a different taste. Again, this is an easy little sauce that works well with barbecued or pan-fried fish, meat or poultry — for that matter, it's great over steamed or boiled vegetables, as well.

4 x 185 g (6½ oz) pieces snapper fillet, skin on
extra virgin olive oil
sea salt and freshly ground pepper
1 lemon

green olive and tomato sauce
250 g (9 oz) green olives, pitted and chopped
400 g (14 oz) tinned whole roma (plum) tomatoes,
    juice reserved, roughly chopped
3 tablespoons extra virgin olive oil
3 garlic cloves, finely chopped
½ teaspoon chilli flakes
3 tablespoons salted baby capers, rinsed
sea salt
1 tablespoon thyme leaves

Serves 4

Scrape the back of a knife backwards and forwards over the snapper skin to remove moisture; this will help the skin become crisp.

Next, make the sauce. In a saucepan over medium heat add the oil, garlic and chilli flakes. Cook for about 3 minutes until the garlic turns golden but does not burn. Add the tomatoes and their juice, olives and capers. Season with a little salt and simmer uncovered for about 15 minutes, or until the sauce begins to thicken. Add the thyme leaves and check the seasoning; adjust if need be.

Drizzle the fish with oil and sprinkle with sea salt. Heat a chargrill pan or barbecue to hot. Add the fish, skin side down, and cook for about 3 minutes, then turn and cook for a further minute, or until cooked. Rest in a warm place for 1 minute. Place a spoonful of sauce on each plate, top with the fish, drizzle with oil, and give a sprinkle of sea salt, a grind of pepper and a squeeze of lemon. Serve at once.

Great with: Steamed spinach and roast potatoes (page 242).

I would ask you to simply use the recipes in this book to cook some delicious dishes, but most importantly, to use them as inspiration. Chop and change ingredients to suit your mood, likes and dislikes, and of course what is at your disposal to cook in the first place. Braised quail could easily be chook, any fish you choose is likely to suit any of the sauces and garnishes, and all the pasta dishes could, minus the pasta, make amazing sauces for lots of fish, poultry or meats. Developing good cooking skills puts you in the driver's seat, so go in peace and cook beautiful food.

Grilled blue eye with garlic and anchovy butter This is a simple fish dish with heaps of flavour. The compound butter goes well with any grilled (broiled), roasted or barbecued food. It can also be whisked into a sauté with the pan juices and a little wine or water to make a great sauce. This butter makes more than enough for four people — it is hard to make any less in the food processor, but it is easy to make the butter and pop the surplus in the freezer, then whenever you want to add flavour to your food, presto. Blue eye today, roast chicken with garlic butter tomorrow.

4 x 185 g (6½ oz) pieces blue eye fillet, skin removed
extra virgin olive oil
sea salt and freshly ground pepper
1 lemon

garlic butter (makes 250 g/9 oz/1 cup)
250 g (9 oz/1 cup) unsalted butter, softened
8 garlic cloves, finely chopped
6 anchovies, finely chopped
2 tablespoons chopped flat-leaf (Italian) parsley
juice of 1 lemon
sea salt and freshly ground pepper

Serves 4

To make the garlic butter, process all the ingredients until just combined, then adjust the seasoning to taste. Roll the mixture in a sheet of baking paper into a log, about 35 cm (14 inches) long and 4 cm (1½ inches) in diameter. Wrap in plastic wrap and refrigerate until firm. Cut the butter into 1 cm (½ inch) thick rounds and allow to come to room temperature. Alternatively, keep out the amount of butter you are using for this dish and simply put a teaspoon on top of each piece of fish to melt into it; it's a bit more rustic than the slices — you choose. But don't forget to refrigerate or freeze the rest.

Heat a grill (broiler), barbecue or frying pan to hot. Drizzle a little oil on the blue eye fillets and sprinkle with sea salt. Cook the fish for 2 minutes, depending on the thickness, then, when well crusted, turn and cook for a further minute. Remove and rest for a minute. Place each piece of fish on a plate and top with a round of butter, then season with sea salt, freshly ground pepper and a squeeze of lemon juice.

Note: This is awesome with boiled green beans and potatoes.

Snapper tagine Here is another classic dish that I often cook at home. I'm really addicted to the flavours of Morocco and this tagine is quite simple to put together. Once you are used to making chermoula, you will use it to make all manner of tagines. Vary the spice mix, the protein and the dried fruits and nuts, as well as the olives you add. This basic recipe can morph into dozens of beautiful braises with a little imagination.

4 x 185 g (6½ oz) pieces snapper fillet, skin on
125 ml (4 fl oz/½ cup) chermoula (see below)
extra virgin olive oil
12 cherry tomatoes, halved
2 red capsicums (peppers), roasted, peeled and sliced
    into strips (page 176)
1 large sweet potato, diced and steamed
4 fresh dates, halved lengthways, seeds removed
1 small handful black olives
400 ml (14 fl oz) chicken stock (page 245)
couscous (page 244)
harissa (page 245)

chermoula (makes about 250 ml/9 fl oz/1 cup)
1 small red onion, roughly chopped
2 garlic cloves, roughly chopped
1 large handful flat-leaf (Italian) parsley leaves and
    stalks, roughly chopped
1 large handful coriander (cilantro) leaves and stalks,
    roughly chopped
2 teaspoons ground cumin
2 teaspoons ground turmeric
2 teaspoons ground chilli
1 teaspoon paprika
½ teaspoon sea salt
80 ml (2½ fl oz/⅓ cup) extra virgin olive oil
juice of ½ lemon

Serves 4

To make the chermoula, process all the ingredients, except the oil and lemon juice, until well combined. Gradually add the oil until a thick paste forms. Stir through the lemon juice.

For the tagine, smear 1 tablespoon of chermoula over the skin of each snapper fillet. Heat some oil in a deep heavy-based frying pan, add the snapper, chermoula side down, and cook until the chermoula is fragrant and starting to colour. Add the tomato, capsicum, sweet potato, dates, olives, stock and remaining chermoula to the pan. Bring the liquid to just below simmering point and cook, covered, over low heat, for about 10 minutes, or until the fish is just cooked through. Check the seasoning and serve with couscous and harissa.

Store any leftover chermoula in an airtight container in the fridge — it will keep for a good 3–4 weeks.

Garam masala braised chicken This chicken dish is inspired by a great Rockpool fish dish, and is so delicious you will make it all the time. The trick (well, it isn't really a trick, it's just good cooking) is to caramelize the aromatics until you smell a wonderful cooked aroma of onions, garlic and ginger. Your braise will then have amazing complexity.

1 large organic chicken, about 2 kg (4 lb 8 oz)
vegetable oil
2 small red onions, sliced
6 garlic cloves, sliced
6 cm (2 1/2 inch) piece ginger, peeled and thinly sliced
6 small hot chillies, finely chopped
sea salt
30 g (1 oz) garam masala
1 tablespoon ground turmeric
1 tablespoon sweet paprika
360 ml (12 fl oz) tin coconut milk
fish sauce
grated palm sugar (jaggery)
juice of 2 lemons
3 tablespoons coconut cream
1 small handful Thai basil leaves
1 small handful coriander (cilantro) leaves

Serves 4

Put the chicken on a chopping board and remove the wing tips. Remove the legs and cut the thighs and drumsticks in half. Remove the backbone to leave the breasts and wings on the double ribcage. Cut down the centre to separate the two breasts and cut each breast into three pieces.

Heat a little vegetable oil in a large pan and brown the chicken pieces well on all sides, working in batches if need be. Remove from the pan and set aside.

Add the onion, garlic, ginger, chilli and a good pinch of salt to the same pan and sauté over low heat for about 15 minutes, constantly stirring, until the vegetables and spices are soft. Add the garam masala, turmeric and sweet paprika and fry for a further minute. Add the coconut milk and 500 ml (17 fl oz/2 cups) water, then season with fish sauce and palm sugar, to taste.

Return the chicken pieces to the pan and simmer, covered, at a very low temperature for 30–45 minutes, or until just cooked. Stir through the lemon juice, coconut cream, basil and coriander leaves. Divide among four bowls and serve with rice and a spoon for the broth.

Chicken braised in coconut milk with whole spices

This is the simplest fresh curry imaginable. You can use the same sauce and simmer any seafood and it will be equally good.

750 g (1 lb 10 oz) boneless, skinless chicken thigh, trimmed and halved
1 tablespoon peeled and finely chopped ginger
4 garlic cloves, roughly chopped
4 French shallots, roughly chopped
2 teaspoons ground cumin
2 teaspoons ground coriander
1/4 teaspoon ground turmeric
1 teaspoon sea salt
400 ml (14 fl oz) coconut milk
40 ml (1¼ fl oz) vegetable oil
4 star anise
6 cardamom pods, bruised
2 dried long red chillies
4 cloves
2 cinnamon sticks
20 fresh curry leaves
250 ml (9 fl oz/1 cup) chicken stock (page 245)
2 bintje (yellow finn) or other waxy potatoes, peeled and cut into 2 cm (3/4 inch) dice
12 green beans or 6 asparagus spears, trimmed and halved
2 tablespoons grated palm sugar (jaggery)
2 tablespoons fish sauce
juice of 2 limes

Serves 4

Blend or process the ginger, garlic and shallots together until smooth. Add the cumin, coriander, turmeric, salt and coconut milk and blend until well combined.

Heat the oil in a heavy-based saucepan over medium heat. Add the star anise, cardamom, chillies, cloves, cinnamon and curry leaves and cook, stirring, for 1 minute, or until the spices are fragrant. Add half the coconut mixture, bring to the boil and add the chicken. Simmer for 5 minutes, or until the oil splits and comes to the surface. Add the remaining coconut mixture with the chicken stock, reduce the heat to a low simmer, and cook uncovered for 30 minutes. Add the potato and beans or asparagus, cover with a lid and cook for a further 15 minutes, or until the vegetables are tender.

Remove and discard the whole spices, then add the palm sugar, fish sauce and lime juice. Taste and adjust the seasonings if necessary. Serve with steamed jasmine rice (page 244).

Chicken cacciatore

Chicken cacciatore This is a nice little braise to throw together. It is also really good to make when you have some spare time, such as on the weekend, and then reheat a couple of days later. Heat it up after you get home from work, take the cork out of a good bottle and you have a great winter evening's meal.

4 boneless chicken thigh fillets, about 750 g (1 lb 10 oz), with skin on
10 g (¼ oz) dried porcini mushrooms
3 tablespoons extra virgin olive oil
sea salt
1 small onion, finely chopped
1 small carrot, finely chopped
1 small celery stalk, finely chopped
6 garlic cloves, finely chopped
250 g (9 oz) small Swiss brown mushrooms, halved and thickly sliced
250 g (9 oz) large field mushrooms, roughly chopped
2 teaspoons plain (all-purpose) flour
250 ml (9 fl oz/1 cup) quality red wine
400 g (14 oz) tinned roma (plum) tomatoes, juice reserved, chopped
2 rosemary sprigs
freshly ground pepper

Serves 4

Soak the dried porcini in 125 ml (4 fl oz/½ cup) boiling water for 30 minutes. Drain and roughly chop the mushrooms; reserve the soaking liquid.

Heat 2 tablespoons of the oil in a large casserole or deep sauté pan over medium heat. Season the chicken on both sides with a little salt and add to the pan, skin side down. Cook until golden on both sides, then remove the chicken and its juices from the pan and set aside.

Heat the remaining oil in the same pan and cook the onion, carrot and celery over low–medium heat for about 10 minutes, or until very soft. Add the garlic and cook for a further 5 minutes. Remove the vegetables from the pan.

Add the fresh mushrooms to the pan and cook, stirring, for about 5 minutes, or until tender. Add the porcini, reserved vegetables and flour to the mushrooms and cook, stirring, for about 2 minutes. Add the red wine and cook, stirring until the liquid boils, and reduces by about half. Stir the tomato and its juice and the reserved porcini liquid through the sauce and then return the chicken to the pan. Add the rosemary sprigs, cover, and simmer gently for about 20 minutes, or until the chicken is cooked through. Remove the rosemary sprigs. Taste and adjust the seasoning if necessary.

Great with: Soft polenta (page 243) and boiled green beans.

Pan-fried chicken breast with tzatziki

Try the tzatziki on any barbecued food. It is a simple but wonderful accompaniment and is great as a dip with some crusty bread.

4 chicken breasts, skin on, flattened with a meat mallet
extra virgin olive oil
1 tablespoon unsalted butter
sea salt and freshly ground pepper
1 tablespoon roughly chopped dill

tzatziki
1/2 Lebanese (short) cucumber, skin on, coarsely grated
250 g (9 oz/1 cup) sheep's milk yoghurt
juice of 1/2 lemon
sea salt and freshly ground pepper
2 garlic cloves, crushed
2 tablespoons finely shredded mint

Serves 4

To make the tzatziki, place the cucumber in a sieve or colander over a bowl and stand for 30 minutes. Press down on the cucumber to extract as much liquid as possible. Discard the juices from the bowl. Combine the yoghurt with the lemon juice, salt and lots of freshly ground pepper. Ad the cucumber and garlic. Check the balance and finish by adding the mint.

Heat a little oil in a pan. When the oil is hot, add the butter and when nut brown, add the seasoned chicken breasts, skin side down. Cook for 3 minutes, turn over, and cook a further 3 minutes on the other side. Remove from the pan and rest the chicken in a warm oven for 10 minutes. You may need to cook the chicken in two batches if you don't have a big enough pan.

Divide the chicken among four large plates, place a spoonful of tzatziki over each breast, sprinkle with chopped dill, and give a good grind of fresh pepper and a drizzle of oil.

Great with: Roast potatoes (page 242) and boiled green beans. I also really love the flavour of corn with the chicken and yoghurt.

Saffron chicken and rice This is a great one-pot dish. Just brown the chicken, chuck everything in and forget it. I often make variations of this dish at home and more often than not add a teaspoon of chilli flakes. Love it hot!

1 kg (2 lb 4 oz) boneless chicken thighs, skin on, halved
500 g (1 lb 2 oz/2¹/₂ cups) long-grain rice
750 ml (24 fl oz/3 cups) chicken stock (page 245)
1¹/₂ teaspoons saffron threads
3 bay leaves, fresh if available
3 cloves
sea salt and freshly ground pepper
2 tablespoons olive oil
1 onion, finely diced
1 green capsicum (pepper), seeds removed and finely diced
3 garlic cloves, finely chopped
¹/₂ teaspoon ground cumin
¹/₂ teaspoon ground coriander
¹/₂ teaspoon ground fennel
400 g (14 oz) tinned diced tomatoes
150 g (5¹/₂ oz/1 cup) freshly shelled peas, about 350 g (12 oz) unshelled

Serves 4

Pour the stock into a saucepan and bring to a simmer over medium–high heat. Reduce the heat to low and add the saffron threads, bay leaves and cloves. Cover the saucepan with a tight-fitting lid and keep the broth warm over low heat.

Season the chicken on both sides with salt and pepper. Heat the oil in a deep, heavy-based frying pan and add the chicken, skin side down. Cook until golden on both sides, then remove from the pan. Reduce the heat and add the onion, capsicum and garlic to the pan with a little extra salt and cook, stirring occasionally, until the vegetables are soft. Add the ground spices and rice and cook, stirring, until the rice is well coated in oil and the spices are fragrant. Pour in the stock, tomatoes and their juice and peas, bring to a simmer and stir again.

Arrange the chicken over the rice and cover the pan with a tight-fitting lid. Reduce the heat to very low and cook, covered, for 15 minutes. Turn off the heat and allow to stand, covered, for a further 10 minutes. Remove the lid and check the seasoning. Discard the bay leaves and cloves before serving. Divide among four large bowls and serve with a green salad.

Barbecued marinated chicken with tabouleh

Easy to throw together and full of flavour, this marinade can be used on any meat or fish, and the tabouleh will be great as a side dish, or served on the plate. I often cook this dish at home, and love to serve it with a little seasoned yoghurt on top.

4 whole chicken legs, drumstick and thigh separated
extra virgin olive oil
1 lemon
freshly ground pepper

marinade
100 ml (3½ fl oz) extra virgin olive oil
4 garlic cloves
juice of ½ lemon
2 teaspoons ground coriander
2 teaspoons ground cumin
3 small red chillies, roughly chopped
3 thyme sprigs, leaves picked
sea salt

tabouleh
140 g (5 oz/heaped ¾ cup) coarse burghul (bulgar)
2 vine-ripened tomatoes, peeled, seeds removed
    and chopped (page 19)
1 Lebanese (short) cucumber, seeds removed and
    chopped
6 spring onions (scallions), chopped
½ bunch parsley, stalks only, about 75 g (2½ oz),
    chopped
1 large handful flat-leaf (Italian) parsley leaves,
    roughly chopped
1 small handful mint leaves, roughly chopped
1 garlic clove, finely chopped
100 ml (3½ fl oz) extra virgin olive oil
juice of 1 lemon
sea salt and freshly ground pepper

Serves 4

Process all the marinade ingredients together until well combined. Add the chicken pieces to the marinade, mix well and refrigerate for 2 hours.

Meanwhile, to make the tabouleh, soak the burghul in a bowl with enough water to cover for at least 1 hour. Drain and squeeze out the excess water. Add the remaining ingredients and mix well.

Heat a barbecue to hot, then place the chicken on, skin side down. Cook for 5 minutes and turn, cook for a further 5 minutes and then remove to a warm oven to rest for 5 minutes.

Spoon the tabouleh onto each of four plates, and place a thigh and a drumstick on each plate. Drizzle with oil, squeeze over some lemon and give a generous grind of fresh pepper.

Roast split chicken with marinade under the skin This is a quick way to roast a chook, with delicious results as the butter melts and moistens the chicken meat, leaving all the flavour of spices and herbs under the skin. Splitting the chicken is a great way to cook it even without the stuffing, so you can just drizzle with oil and sprinkle both inside and out with sea salt. Roast, rest and add lemon juice and you have a wonderful roast chook. This is also a great preparation for barbecuing whole birds. You can replace the chicken with two spatchcocks if you prefer.

1.5 kg (3 lb 5 oz) corn-fed chicken
5 garlic cloves, poached in salted water for 5 minutes, then peeled
sea salt
1 handful coriander (cilantro) leaves, roughly chopped
1 handful flat-leaf (Italian) parsley leaves, roughly chopped
1½ teaspoons ground cumin
grated zest of 1 lemon
1½ teaspoons saffron threads, soaked in 2 tablespoons hot water
150 g (5½ oz) unsalted butter, softened
extra virgin olive oil
1 lemon
freshly ground pepper

Serves 2

Preheat the oven to 200°C (400°F/Gas 6). Butterfly the chicken by splitting it down the backbone and pushing down on the breastbone to flatten it. Pull the skin back on the breast to release it from the flesh and create a pocket under the skin. Be careful not to tear the skin at this point.

Pound the poached garlic and salt in a mortar with a pestle to form a paste, then add the coriander, parsley, cumin, lemon zest, and saffron and its soaking water. Add the butter and mix thoroughly. Force the pounded butter mixture under the chicken skin and into the legs and over the breasts, then smooth out. Season the chicken with salt and drizzle with oil.

Heat some oil in a large ovenproof frying pan. Add the chicken to the pan, breast side down, and colour it for a couple of minutes. Turn the chicken and place the pan in the hot oven for 20 minutes. Remove the pan from the oven and rest the chicken in a warm place for a further 15 minutes.

Squeeze the juice from the lemon into the pan and mix with the cooking juices. Carve the legs and thighs from the chicken and cut the breasts into two or three pieces each. Pour the juices over the chicken. Give a really good grind of fresh pepper.

Great with: Roast potatoes (page 242) and a bowl of mixed steamed greens.

Sauté of chicken with balsamic-braised radicchio and aïoli

I love caramelized chicken skin with aïoli and I love cooked radicchio — so this dish is a favourite. I would definitely serve it with potato gratin ... even those who say they don't like potato eat potato gratin with great relish.

4 single chicken breasts with wing bone attached and skin intact
extra virgin olive oil
sea salt
aïoli (page 246)
freshly ground pepper

balsamic-braised radicchio
125 ml (4 fl oz/1/2 cup) extra virgin olive oil
2 radicchio, washed gently and quartered lengthways
2 tablespoons balsamic vinegar
sea salt and freshly ground pepper

Serves 4

To make the balsamic-braised radicchio, heat half the oil in a large frying pan over medium–high heat. Add the radicchio and cook until starting to brown. Turn over and cook until browned on the other side, then drizzle with the remaining oil and the balsamic vinegar. Season with sea salt and cook for a further minute, or until the radicchio has wilted and the liquid has reduced. Remove and give a good grind of pepper.

Drizzle the chicken with oil and sea salt. Heat a large heavy-based pan over medium–high heat, add the chicken, skin side down, and cook for 5 minutes until golden. Turn over and cook for a further 4 minutes. Remove and place in a warm oven to rest for 5 minutes.

Place the chicken on four plates with the radicchio and a dollop of aïoli. Finish with a good grind of pepper and serve, of course, with potato gratin (page 241).

Quail braised in red wine

This is a great way to braise quail, but by all means if you don't have an oven, or in fact don't feel like using it, just cook on top of the stove on a gentle simmer. I love the way the flesh simply falls off the bone … you just shred it with your spoon or fork and don't even have to pick the bones up with your fingers. Spatchcock or duck legs cooked in the same way are also fantastic.

8 quail
sea salt
3 tablespoons extra virgin olive oil
1 red onion, quartered
8 garlic cloves
1 tablespoon ginger, peeled and cut into julienne
2 rosemary sprigs
4 thyme sprigs
2 dried long red chillies, seeds removed and crushed
2 carrots, sliced into 1 cm (1/2 inch) thick rounds
250 ml (9 fl oz/1 cup) quality red wine
400 g (14 oz) tinned tomatoes, juice reserved
150 ml (5 fl oz) chicken stock (page 245)
freshly ground pepper

Serves 4

Season the quail inside and out with sea salt. Preheat the oven to 160°C (315°F/Gas 2–3).

Heat the oil in a large heavy-based, ovenproof pan. Add the quail to the pan, two or three at a time, and brown well on all sides. Remove from the pan and set aside. Add the onion, garlic, ginger, rosemary, thyme, chilli and carrot and sauté for 2 minutes, or until starting to soften. Add the wine and simmer until reduced. Add the tomato and its juice, stock and quail, breast side down, season to taste and bring to the boil. Cover with a tight-fitting lid and place in the oven. Cook for 40 minutes.

Remove the pan from the oven, gently turn the quail over, return the pan to the oven and cook, uncovered, for a further 10 minutes, or until well browned. Remove from the oven; the quail should be almost falling apart. Check the seasoning of the sauce and adjust if necessary. Spoon two quail into each of the pasta bowls, pour over the sauce and give a generous grind of pepper before serving.

Great with: Soft polenta (page 243) and snow peas (mangetout); otherwise, it is also great with rice or some small pasta like risoni.

Duck braised with white beans I love this dish. It can be changed around by adding pork sausage, duck confit or belly pork. You can also add some breadcrumbs over the beans with about an hour to go, then dot with butter and you will create a cassoulet effect.

4 large duck legs
250 g (9 oz) white beans, soaked overnight, then
    drained
250 g (9 oz) pancetta, cut into 4 pieces
400 g (14 oz) tinned whole tomatoes, puréed
4 garlic cloves
1 onion, chopped roughly
115 g (4 oz/$1/3$ cup) dark molasses
60 g ($2^1/4$ oz/$1/3$ cup) brown sugar
2 teaspoons dijon mustard
$1^1/2$ teaspoons ground ginger
sea salt

Serves 4

Preheat the oven to 140°C (275°F/Gas 1). Cut the duck legs down the centre to separate the thigh and drumstick.

Put the beans into a large saucepan and cover with cold water. Bring to a simmer and cook for 5 minutes, skimming any scum that rises to the top. Drain the beans and rinse. Place the beans in a Dutch oven with a tight-fitting lid (or a heavy-based stewing pan with lid). Add the duck pieces, pancetta, puréed tomato, whole garlic cloves, onion, molasses, sugar, mustard, ginger and sea salt and stir well. Add about 375 ml (13 fl oz/ $1^1/2$ cups) water to just cover, put the lid on, and put in the oven for 2 hours. Remove the lid and bake for 3 more hours. A nice crust should form and the beans should be tender and the meat soft. Place a duck thigh and drumstick and pancetta piece on each plate and top with beans.

Great with: A big green salad dressed with extra virgin olive oil and red wine vinegar; you will be in heaven. It is so rich that anything else would be overkill.

Honey-braised duck with orange and olives

This is a really delicious dish, where the oven does all the work for you. Many people seem to steer clear of cooking duck at home. Make this and it will change your mind. Buying legs is the easiest way, but by all means chop up a whole duck and go full steam ahead.

4 large duck legs
2 tablespoons extra virgin olive oil
8 French shallots, halved lengthways if large
500 ml (17 fl oz/2 cups) chicken stock (page 245)
2 tablespoons honey (such as leatherwood or other strong-flavoured honey)
1/2 teaspoon ground cinnamon
1/2 teaspoon ground coriander
6 garlic cloves
1 rosemary sprig, leaves only
1 orange, segmented (page 83)
180 g (6 1/2 oz) green olives
sea salt and freshly ground pepper
30 ml (1 fl oz) freshly squeezed orange juice

Serves 4

Preheat the oven to 200°C (400°F/Gas 6). Cut the duck legs in half at the joint and remove all the bones, keeping the meat intact as much as possible. Heat the oil in a deep, ovenproof, heavy-based frying pan until it smokes. Add the duck, skin side down, and brown for about 2 minutes per side. Remove the duck from the pan and set aside.

Add the shallots to the pan and toss until golden, then remove and reserve them. Discard the rendered duck fat. Add the stock, stirring to loosen any caramelized bits from the bottom of the pan. Stir in the honey and spices, place the duck back in, skin side up, along with the shallots, garlic, rosemary, orange segments, olives and seasoning. Bring to the boil.

Transfer the pan to the oven and cook for 10 minutes. Reduce the temperature to 180°C (350°F/Gas 4), cover with a tight-fitting lid or several layers of foil and cook for a further 30 minutes.

Strain the duck mixture through a fine sieve into a large bowl and reserve the solids. Return the liquid to the pan and simmer, uncovered, to reduce it slightly. Skim any impurities from the top. Add the orange juice to the pan with the reserved solids and check the seasoning.

Great with: Couscous (page 244) or rice and a salad.

Pan-fried duck with cherry tomato and oregano vinaigrette

This vinaigrette works nicely with meat and poultry, as well as seafood. Try barbecuing the duck breast to add a nice smoky flavour to the dish.

4 duck breasts, skin on
sea salt
extra virgin olive oil
freshly ground pepper

cherry tomato and oregano vinaigrette
1/4 red onion, finely chopped
1 garlic clove, finely chopped
sea salt
250 g (9 oz) cherry tomatoes, quartered
2 tablespoons oregano leaves
100 ml (3½ fl oz) extra virgin olive oil, plus extra, to sauté
3 teaspoons balsamic vinegar
freshly ground pepper

Serves 4

To make the vinaigrette, heat some oil in a pan and sauté the onion and garlic with a little salt until soft. Add the tomato and simmer slowly for 10 minutes. Remove from the heat, stir in the oregano, oil and balsamic vinegar and season with sea salt and freshly ground pepper.

Season the duck breasts with some sea salt and place, skin side down, in a hot pan with some oil. Cook over medium–high heat for 5 minutes, or until the skin turns golden, then turn over and cook for another 3 minutes. Allow to rest for 10 minutes in a warm oven.

To serve, slice the breasts thinly and place on four large plates. Spoon the vinaigrette over and give another grind of fresh pepper.

Great with: Yam purée and buttered brussels sprouts. I love brussels sprouts and if you cook them properly, everyone else will love them too.

Barbecued pork sausages with balsamic onion sauce This is a classic dish that relies on the quality of the pork sausage. The sauce works well with any barbecued meat, or of course you could just pan-fry the sausages.

8 fat pork sausages
sea salt
extra virgin olive oil
freshly ground pepper

balsamic onion sauce
2 tablespoons olive oil
3 large red onions, halved and thinly sliced
100 ml (3½ fl oz) balsamic vinegar
30 g (1 oz) unsalted butter
1 teaspoon sea salt
2 teaspoons caster (superfine) sugar
125 ml (4 fl oz/½ cup) chicken stock (page 245)

Serves 4

To make the sauce, heat the olive oil in a heavy-based frying pan over medium heat. Add the onion, reduce the heat to low and cook, covered, for 10 minutes, or until very soft. Remove the lid, increase the heat to medium and continue to cook the onion, stirring occasionally, until it begins to brown. Add the vinegar and simmer until almost completely evaporated. Reduce the heat to low again, add the butter, sea salt, sugar and stock and stir well. Simmer for a further 3–4 minutes, or until the flavours have combined and the sauce is thick and syrupy.

Season the sausages with sea salt and drizzle with oil, then cook on a hot barbecue until golden brown on all sides. Place two sausages on each plate with a heaped spoonful of the balsamic onion sauce (the sauce can be served warm or at room temperature). Give a good grind of fresh pepper and serve.

Great with: Potato purée (page 243) and salad.

Crumbed pork cutlet with sautéed apples, potatoes and sage

A great friend of mine says, 'If you want to sell it, crumb it'. He is of course referring to the obsession we all seem to have with crispy food. I have never met anyone who didn't like schnitzel, and this crumbed cutlet is a form of schnitzel. Here, as always, I'm suggesting you take the high road and make your own breadcrumbs, but if you don't want to, just use the bought variety and the result will still be very satisfying. If you can get your hands on some beautiful small kipflers (fingerlings), leave them whole in this recipe. If, instead, you are using pink eyes or similar, you may want to cut them in half after steaming.

4 pork cutlets, lightly pounded with a meat mallet
    to flatten slightly
60 g (2¼ oz/½ cup) plain (all-purpose) flour
sea salt
3 tablespoons milk
1 egg
120 g (4¼ oz/1½ cups) day-old white breadcrumbs,
    dried slightly in the oven
80 ml (2½ fl oz/⅓ cup) extra virgin olive oil
60 g (2¼ oz/¼ cup) unsalted butter
lemon wedges

sautéed apples, potatoes and sage
2 Granny Smith apples, peeled, cored and cut into
    sixths
300 g (10½ oz) small waxy potatoes, such as pink
    eye or kifpler (fingerling), steamed for 20 minutes
    and peeled
2 garlic cloves, crushed
10–12 sage leaves
80 ml (2½ fl oz/⅓ cup) extra virgin olive oil
30 g (1 oz) unsalted butter, plus 1 tablespoon extra
3 tablespoons white wine
3 tablespoons chicken stock (page 245)
sea salt and freshly ground pepper

Serves 4

Place the flour on a flat plate and season with some sea salt. Whisk the milk and egg together in a bowl. Place the breadcrumbs on a separate flat plate. Dip the pork cutlets in the seasoned flour and shake away any excess flour, then dip into the combined milk and egg. Finish by dipping the cutlets into the breadcrumbs, ensuring the meat and bone are evenly coated. Shake away any excess breadcrumbs.

Heat half the oil and butter in a frying pan. When the butter is foaming, add two pork cutlets and cook over medium heat until the breadcrumbs are golden. Turn and cook the other side until golden and the pork is just cooked. Place in a warm oven and repeat the process with the remaining two cutlets.

Heat a pan over medium heat, and sauté the apple, potato, garlic and sage leaves in the oil and butter. When the butter is nut brown, add the wine and cook for 2 minutes, then add the stock and cook for a further 2 minutes. Add the extra butter to the pan, remove from the heat and swirl to incorporate. Season with sea salt and freshly ground pepper.

Place a chop on each plate, some sautéed potato and apples next to it and serve with a wedge of lemon.

Braised pork with chillies I love anything with pork belly in it. The good thing about it is if you give it a really good fry first, that will render out a lot of the fat, so I guess in a way it is a little healthy ... who am I kidding? It just tastes good!

1 kg (2 lb 4 oz) pork belly, cut into 5 x 8 cm
    (2 x 3¼ inch) pieces
2 tablespoons unsalted butter
olive oil
sea salt
5 dried long red chillies
3 garlic cloves, roughly chopped
1 teaspoon ground cumin
2 bay leaves, fresh if available
1 piece of orange rind

Serves 4

Melt the butter and a splash of oil in a wide pan over medium heat. Put the pork belly into the pan in a single layer and season with sea salt. Cook the pork slowly, for about 30 minutes, turning occasionally, until the meat is golden brown and most of the fat has been rendered. Pour off and discard most of the fat.

Meanwhile, put the chillies in a bowl with 500 ml (17 fl oz/2 cups) boiling water and allow to soak for about 30 minutes. Remove the chillies, reserving the water, and chop roughly. Blend or process the chillies, garlic, cumin and the chilli water until smooth.

Add the chilli sauce, bay leaves and orange rind to the pork and stir with a wooden spoon, scraping any brown bits stuck to the bottom of the pan. Reduce the heat to low, cover and braise the meat for about 1½ hours, or until it is very tender and the sauce has thickened. Remove the bay leaves and orange rind and adjust the seasoning if necessary. Divide the pork among four large bowls and serve with steamed jasmine rice (page 244).

Barbecued lamb cutlets in green masala

This simple marinade will enhance the flavour of meat and fish. It works well on the barbecue, but by all means just pan-fry, or even marinate and roast larger cuts of meat.

12 lamb cutlets
1 teaspoon fennel seeds
1 teaspoon coriander seeds
8 cardamom pods, seeds removed and pods discarded
sea salt
1 large handful coriander (cilantro) leaves
1 large handful mint leaves
1 teaspoon ground chilli
1 teaspoon ground turmeric
1½ teaspoons garam masala
2 lemons, 1 cut into wedges
2 heaped tablespoons plain yoghurt
extra virgin olive oil
1 large vine-ripened tomato
red wine vinegar
freshly ground pepper

Serves 4

Roast the fennel, coriander and cardamom seeds in a dry frying pan, over medium heat, until fragrant. Place the spices in a mortar, add a pinch of salt and grind the spices to a fine powder using a pestle. You can buy pre-ground spices but they will never match the flavour of whole seeds.

Pound the coriander and mint leaves with a pinch of salt in a mortar with a pestle until broken down. Add the chilli, turmeric, garam masala, freshly ground spices, a further pinch of salt, the juice of 1 lemon and the yoghurt. Mix until well combined. Marinate the cutlets in the spiced yoghurt mixture for about 2 hours.

Heat the barbecue to hot. Brush the bars with a little oil. Add the cutlets and cook for about 3 minutes. Turn over and cook a further 3 minutes. Rest the cutlets in a warm place for about 5 minutes.

Meanwhile, slice the tomato and splash with red wine vinegar and oil. Season with sea salt and freshly ground pepper. Arrange the tomato on four plates, place three lamb cutlets on each plate and serve with a lemon wedge on the side.

Great with: Pumpkin purée (page 181) and steamed green beans.

Chargrilled lamb cutlets with vegetable salsa

This salsa is wonderful with all barbecued, sautéed and roasted food. It adds a lovely texture and flavour to whatever you're cooking. If you are going to barbecue the cutlets, cook all the vegetables on the barbecue as well, which makes the whole thing even easier.

12 lamb cutlets
sea salt
extra virgin olive oil

vegetable salsa
1 red capsicum (pepper)
extra virgin olive oil
1 large zucchini (courgette), cut into 1 cm
    (1/2 inch) dice
1 eggplant (aubergine), sliced into 1 cm (1/2 inch)
    thick rounds
1/2 teaspoon ground cumin
2/3 teaspoon ground fennel
1 tablespoon lemon juice
2 tablespoons chopped basil
2 tablespoons chopped flat-leaf (Italian) parsley
sea salt and freshly ground pepper

Serves 4

Preheat the oven to 220°C (425°F/Gas 7). To make the vegetable salsa, toss the whole capsicum in a little oil and place on a baking tray. Toss the zucchini in a little more oil and place on the same tray. Roast for about 5–10 minutes, or until the zucchini is golden, but still holds its shape. Remove the zucchini from the tray and set aside. Continue to roast the capsicum for a further 10 minutes, or until the skin is starting to blacken and blister. Remove the capsicum from the tray and set aside, covered with plastic wrap, until cool enough to handle. Peel the capsicum, chop the flesh into 1 cm (1/2 inch) pieces and discard the seeds and membrane. Chargrill the eggplant until golden on both sides, cool slightly, then cut into 1 cm (1/2 inch) pieces.

Place the vegetables in a bowl with the ground spices, lemon juice, fresh herbs, a little more oil, sea salt and freshly ground pepper to taste. Toss to combine, then set aside.

Season the cutlets on both sides with salt and drizzle with a little oil. Chargrill the cutlets for 1–2 minutes on each side. Rest for 5 minutes in a warm oven before serving. When ready, place three cutlets on each plate and spoon over the salsa.

Roasted herb-crusted lamb with roasted capsicum sauce The crust adds great texture and flavour and turns a simple dish into something more elegant.

4 x 200 g (7 oz) pieces lamb loin or backstrap
sea salt

herb crust
2 tablespoons chopped flat-leaf (Italian) parsley
1 teaspoon chopped thyme
1 teaspoon chopped rosemary
1 tablespoon chopped chives
3 garlic cloves, finely chopped
1 teaspoon grated lemon zest
50 g (1¾ oz/½ cup) sourdough breadcrumbs
2 tablespoons extra virgin olive oil
sea salt and freshly ground pepper

roasted capsicum sauce
2 small red capsicums (peppers), seeds removed
    and cut into 1.5 cm (⅝ inch) thick strips
1 small red onion, halved
3 long red chillies, halved lengthways and seeds
    removed
2 tablespoons extra virgin olive oil
2 tablespoons white wine
1 tablespoon honey
sea salt

Serves 4

To make the roasted capsicum sauce, preheat the oven to 160°C (315°F/Gas 2–3). Combine the capsicum with the onion and chilli in a roasting pan. Drizzle with the oil, wine and honey, sprinkle over some salt and roast for 1 hour, or until the onion is soft. Purée and check the seasoning.

To make the herb crust, process the herbs, garlic, lemon zest and breadcrumbs until finely chopped. Add the oil, salt and pepper and process until well combined.

Season the lamb loins with sea salt and seal in a hot pan until well browned. Place the loins in a roasting tray and pat a layer of crust on top. Roast at 180°C (350°F/Gas 4) for 15 minutes, or until the crust is golden, then remove from the oven and rest for 10 minutes. On a cutting board, slice the lamb on the diagonal and place each loin on a large plate. Place a spoonful of the chilli-roasted capsicum and onion sauce next to the lamb and serve.

Great with: Potato gratin (page 241) and snow peas (mangetout).

Roast double lamb cutlets with pumpkin purée and rosemary butter

You can leave the racks whole, or cut them into four cutlets if you like. Another thing you could do is remove the lamb from the bone and slice; it will look lovely. Remember that meat cooked on the bone is juicier and more flavourful, so it is worth using the racks rather than the fillets.

4 x 4-bone racks of lamb
sea salt
extra virgin olive oil
freshly ground pepper

pumpkin purée
300 g (10 1/2 oz) peeled pumpkin (winter squash),
    cut into 4 cm (1 1/2 inch) cubes
3 tablespoons unsalted butter
2 teaspoons extra virgin olive oil
sea salt and freshly ground pepper

rosemary butter
1 garlic clove, finely chopped
2 tablespoons chopped flat-leaf (Italian) parsley
1 tablespoon finely chopped rosemary
sea salt
125 g (4 1/2 oz/1/2 cup) unsalted butter, softened
squeeze of lemon juice

Serves 4

Preheat the oven to 180°C (350°F/Gas 4). To make the pumpkin purée, steam the pumpkin for 20–30 minutes until very tender. Purée with the butter and oil until very smooth and light. Season with sea salt and freshly ground pepper.

For the rosemary butter, place the garlic, parsley, rosemary and salt in a mortar and bash with a pestle to form a rough paste. Add the butter and lemon juice and mix to combine. Set aside.

Season the lamb racks with sea salt and seal in a hot pan. Place in the oven and roast for 18 minutes, then remove from the oven and allow to rest in a warm place for at least 10 minutes.

Cut the lamb racks in half to give you eight double cutlets. Place two double cutlets on each large plate, dollop a little rosemary butter on top and serve some pumpkin purée alongside. Give a good grind of pepper, and serve.

Great with: Any of your favourite root vegetable purées, instead of the pumpkin purée, and salad or mixed boiled vegetables drizzled with extra virgin olive oil.

Marinated lamb leg with spicy chargrilled vegetables and garlic yoghurt

Get your butcher to butterfly the leg for you, and avoid the stress of doing it yourself.

1 leg of lamb, de-boned and butterflied
1 lemon
sea salt and freshly ground pepper

marinade
2 tablespoons chopped flat-leaf (Italian) parsley
1 teaspoon chopped thyme
3 garlic cloves, finely chopped
125 ml (4 fl oz/1/2 cup) extra virgin olive oil
1 teaspoon finely grated lemon zest
sea salt

chargrilled vegetables
1 baby fennel, quartered
2 green or yellow zucchini (courgettes), sliced thickly on the diagonal
1 small sweet potato, sliced thickly into rounds
1 red capsicum (pepper), seeds removed and sliced thickly lengthways
1 small red onion, cut into wedges
100 ml (3 1/2 fl oz) extra virgin olive oil
sea salt
3 long red chillies, seeds removed and finely chopped
juice of 1 lemon
freshly ground pepper

yoghurt
250 g (9 oz/1 cup) sheep's milk yoghurt
2 garlic cloves, finely chopped
juice of 1 lemon
sea salt and freshly ground pepper

Serves 4

Combine the marinade ingredients with a little sea salt in a large bowl and mix well. Add the lamb to the bowl and turn a few times to coat well in the marinade. Cover and refrigerate for 6 hours, or overnight, turning occasionally. Remove the lamb from the fridge several hours before cooking.

Preheat the barbecue to hot. Brush the vegetables with a little of the oil and season with sea salt. Chargrill until golden on both sides, then place in a bowl to keep warm. In a mortar, pound the chilli and a little more sea salt with a pestle. Gradually incorporate the remaining oil and lemon juice to form a dressing and season with freshly ground pepper.

Meanwhile, place the lamb on the barbecue and pour over any marinade left in the bowl. Cook for 8 minutes, then turn over and cook for a further 8 minutes. Remove to a plate and allow to rest in a warm oven for 10 minutes.

To make the yoghurt, combine all the ingredients in a bowl and season with salt and pepper to taste.

Dress the vegetables with the dressing in the mortar and divide among four large plates. Carve slices of the lamb leg and top the vegetables with the lamb slices. Add a dollop of yoghurt, a squeeze of lemon and spoon over the juices from the resting plate. Serve.

Great with: Salad and yam purée.

Braised shoulder of lamb with eggplant and tomato jam

Lamb shoulder would have to be my favourite cut of lamb, and the reason is simple: it has lots of connective tissue and that equals flavour. It takes a little time to put this dish together but it is more than worth it.

1.25 kg (2 lb 12 oz) boned lamb shoulder, trimmed of fat
3 garlic cloves, cut into slivers
freshly ground pepper
1 bouquet garni (a few sprigs of thyme and parsley and 1 bay leaf, tied together)
170 ml (5½ fl oz/⅔ cup) white wine
1 tablespoon extra virgin olive oil
sea salt
1 lemon

eggplant and tomato jam
1 large eggplant (aubergine), cut into 1.5 cm (⅝ inch) cubes
750 g (1 lb 10 oz) vine-ripened tomatoes, seeds removed and roughly chopped
80 ml (2½ fl oz/⅓ cup) extra virgin olive oil
1 onion, finely chopped
3 garlic cloves, finely chopped
sea salt
2 bay leaves, fresh if available
1 teaspoon thyme leaves

Serves 4

Lay out the boned shoulder, skin side down. With a small, sharp-pointed knife, pierce the flesh at regular intervals and tuck a sliver of garlic into each vent. Grind over pepper and place in a small, deep dish. Add the bouquet garni, wine and half the oil. Turn the shoulder over and around several times and marinate, covered, for 3–4 hours, turning it a couple of times during that period. Preheat the oven to 230°C (450°F/Gas 8).

Meanwhile, to make the eggplant and tomato jam, warm the oil in a heavy-based frying pan, add the onion and cook over low heat, stirring occasionally until softened. Add the garlic and eggplant and season with salt. Cook, stirring occasionally, until the eggplant begins to soften. Add the tomato and herbs, cover and cook over low heat, stirring occasionally, for 30 minutes, or until the tomato has completely collapsed and the eggplant is very tender. Taste and adjust the seasoning if necessary. Set aside.

Remove the shoulder from the marinade, reserve the marinade and discard the herbs. Pat the shoulder dry with paper towel, then lay it out, skin side down, and sprinkle lightly with salt. Roll the shoulder into a tight cylindrical, melon-type shape and tie it at regular intervals with butcher's string so it holds its shape. This will assist in the even cooking of the shoulder. Rub the surface with the remaining olive oil, sprinkle with salt and place in a small ovenproof pan or casserole dish. Roast for 30 minutes. Reduce the oven temperature to 180°C (350°F/Gas 4).

Remove the lamb from the pan and pour the juices into a jug. Allow the fat to rise to the surface and skim it off. Return the juices to the pan and add the reserved marinade. Place the pan over high heat on the stovetop and bring the mixture to the boil. Return the lamb to the pan and cover with a tight-fitting lid or several layers of foil. Place over low heat and cook for 1 hour, adding 3 tablespoons water to the pan after 30 minutes. Remove the lamb from the pan and increase the heat to high. Boil the liquid, uncovered, until it reduces and becomes syrupy. Add the eggplant and tomato jam and stir to combine. Return the lamb to the pan, and roast in the oven for a final 30 minutes. Remove the lamb from the oven, turn off the heat and leave the door ajar. Cover the lamb with foil and rest in the oven for 20–30 minutes before serving.

To serve, remove the shoulder to a carving board, cut and remove the strings and slice it. Spoon some jam on to each of four plates and top with a few slices of lamb. Give a squeeze of lemon and a grind of fresh pepper.

Roast spring lamb with garlic and rosemary
This is the classic Sunday roast; at least it was when I was growing up. Serve with roasted potatoes (page 242) and boiled green beans — heaven.

2.5 kg (5 lb 8 oz) leg spring lamb, shank on
3 small garlic cloves, each cut lengthways into
    5 thin slices
15 small rosemary sprigs
sea salt
extra virgin olive oil
1 small lemon
freshly ground pepper

Serves 6

Preheat the oven to 220°C (425°F/Gas 7). Remove the lamb from the refrigerator about 2 hours before cooking to allow it to come to room temperature.

Using a sharp thin knife, pierce the lamb in about 15 places (away from the bone), long and deep enough that the garlic slivers will fit in snugly. Insert a piece of garlic into each cut, followed by a piece of rosemary.

Place the lamb in a large roasting tin, salt it well and rub with oil. Cook for 40 minutes. Remove the lamb from the oven, turn the oven off and leave the door slightly ajar. Cover the lamb with foil and return it to the oven to rest for 40 minutes. If using a digital meat thermometer, you want to remove the lamb from the oven at around 53°C (127°F). It will increase to roughly 58°C (136°F) during resting and this should give you perfect medium–rare roasted lamb. For medium, you want a final temperature of 60°C (140°F) and for well done, 65°C (149°F).

Once rested, remove the lamb from the oven and transfer to a cutting board. Place the roasting tin on the stove, squeeze the lemon into the pan juices, add 1 tablespoon oil and stir through. Leave on a very low heat while you carve the lamb.

To carve, position the lamb leg on one of its sides. Holding the shank with a tea towel (dish towel), take a sharp knife and, starting from the ball at the end of the bone, cut down the bone, removing one of the large muscles. Now turn the lamb around and remove the rest of the meat from the bone by cutting down each side of the bone and removing the large piece of muscle left. You should have two large pieces of meat on the board that you can now cut into slices. Place the piece from near the bone on the board and slice straight down, as if you were going down the length of the leg bone. This will give you semi-circular pieces that will be across the grain, making the lamb more tender. You can cut the shank off now and fight over who gets to eat it. Place 3–5 slices on each plate or serve on a large platter. Spoon the roasting juices over the top, give a good grind of fresh pepper and serve immediately with a delicious, simple radicchio salad of finely shredded radicchio leaves, tossed with extra virgin olive oil, balsamic vinegar, sea salt and freshly ground pepper.

Great with: You have to roast some vegetables with this; it is the only way to go.

Veal involtini with simple fresh tomato sauce This dish is very quick to cook and put together. The most important thing is not to overcook the veal or to stew the tomato sauce too much. It is the fresh taste that makes it perfect.

12 small pieces veal rump or topside, about 80 g
    (2³/4 oz) each, beaten into thin steaks
12 sage leaves
6 anchovies, halved lengthways
1 tablespoon finely chopped thyme
sea salt
extra virgin olive oil
freshly ground pepper
1 tablespoon chopped flat-leaf (Italian) parsley

tomato sauce
8 roma (plum) tomatoes, seeds removed and finely
    chopped
2 tablespoons extra virgin olive oil
2 garlic cloves, chopped
1 small red onion, roughly diced
sea salt

Serves 4

To make the tomato sauce, heat a little oil in a pan and sauté the garlic and onion with a little sea salt until the onion is soft. Add the tomato and sauté for about 5 minutes, or until the tomato just starts to break up. You want the tomato to retain some of its texture.

Lay out the veal pieces and place 1 sage leaf, half an anchovy and a little thyme on each. Roll the veal pieces up loosely and thread toothpicks through the ends to hold them together. Season the veal well with sea salt.

Heat a little oil in a frying pan or casserole dish over medium heat. Add the veal to the pan in batches, and cook until browned on both sides and cooked to your liking — this will only take a few minutes. Return all the meat to the pan, add the tomato sauce and gently warm it through. Give a good grind of fresh pepper.

Remove the toothpicks and place three involtinis on each plate. Spoon over some sauce, sprinkle with parsley, drizzle with oil and serve.

Great with: Potato purée (page 243) and sugar snap peas.

Veal schnitzel with coleslaw

This is the classic schnitzel, and yes, I love it with coleslaw. If you don't want the slaw tossed in mayonnaise, just dress it with extra virgin olive oil and red wine vinegar. In many ways I like it that way — Italian style — more than I do the mayo version. Again, just buy breadcrumbs if you don't have time to make them yourself.

4 x 165 g (5¾ oz) pieces veal schnitzel (flattened rump or topside)
2 tablespoons milk
1 egg
sea salt
60 g (2¼ oz/½ cup) plain (all-purpose) flour
165 g (5¾ oz/2 cups) day-old white breadcrumbs, dried slightly in the oven
3 tablespoons olive oil
3 tablespoons unsalted butter
lemon wedges

coleslaw
¼ Savoy cabbage, very thinly sliced
½ small red onion, very thinly sliced
1 celery stalk, very finely sliced
1 carrot, coarsely grated
60 g (2¼ oz/½ cup) coarsely grated gruyère cheese
125 g (4½ oz/½ cup) aïoli (page 246)

Serves 4

To make the coleslaw, place all the ingredients in a large bowl and toss to combine.

To make the schnitzel, place the milk and egg in a shallow bowl, season with salt and whisk to combine. Place the flour and breadcrumbs on separate flat plates. Dip the veal in the flour and shake away any excess. Dip the floured veal into the egg mixture and allow the excess to drip away. Lastly, coat evenly with the breadcrumbs.

Melt the oil and butter in a large, heavy-based frying pan over medium heat. Cook the veal in batches until golden on both sides, then drain on paper towel.

Divide the schnitzel among four plates and serve with coleslaw and lemon wedges on the side.

Great with: Steamed or boiled potatoes.

Braised veal shanks with polenta

I love sucking on the bones of the veal shanks to get the marrow out. The braise is made lighter by using chicken stock instead of veal stock — I prefer that to a sticky braise.

1.25 kg (2 lb 12 oz) veal shanks, cut osso bucco style
1 tablespoon plain (all-purpose) flour, seasoned with sea salt and freshly ground pepper
extra virgin olive oil
1 onion, finely diced
2 garlic cloves, finely chopped
2 celery stalks, finely diced
2 carrots, finely diced
sea salt
120 g (4¼ oz/1 cup) Ligurian olives
2 tablespoons tomato paste (concentrated purée)
grated zest of 1 lemon
grated zest of 1 orange
250 ml (9 fl oz/1 cup) white wine
400 g (14 oz) tinned tomatoes, juice reserved, roughly chopped
750 ml (26 fl oz/3 cups) chicken stock (page 245)
4 bay leaves, fresh if available
1 thyme sprig
soft polenta (page 243)
freshly ground pepper
1 lemon

Serves 4–6

Toss the veal shanks in the seasoned flour. Heat some oil in a large, heavy-based pan and cook the shanks until browned all over, then remove from the pan. Heat more oil in the pan if necessary and add the onion, garlic, celery, carrot and a pinch of sea salt and cook over medium heat until the onion is soft. Stir in the olives, tomato paste, lemon and orange zests, wine, tomato and its juice, stock, bay leaves, thyme and browned shanks.

Simmer very slowly, covered, for 1 hour. Remove the lid and simmer uncovered for a further 45 minutes, or until the meat is falling off the bone. Check the seasoning and add more sea salt if necessary. Place a spoonful of polenta on the side of four large bowls, spoon the shank mixture on and give a good grind of pepper and a squeeze of fresh lemon.

Great with: Green salad.

I can't imagine eating a beautiful meal without a quality glass of wine. The two to me are complementary and each part lifts the whole to a greater experience. I feel the same whether eating at a great restaurant, or preparing a simple omelette for Sunday lunch at home. The amount of fun that you can have with food and wine is inexhaustible, because there are so many quality wines produced in so many countries around the world. Wine is a living thing and each wine is unique. Drink sensibly and make it an adventure of flavours and great experiences with food. Without becoming a wine snob, it is fun to do tastings, read the odd magazine and even do a course or two. I'm always on the search for the next great food and wine experience. Life is about romance of many kinds, so eat, drink and love well.

Rendang of beef This is probably the simplest curry I know that starts with a fresh paste which you make yourself. It is bloody delicious. Give it a go and I promise you will start to think you're a pretty fine Asian cook.

800 g (1 lb 12 oz) topside beef, cut into cubes
3 tablespoons vegetable oil
150 g (5½ oz) rendang curry paste (see below)
600 ml (21 fl oz) coconut milk
1½ tablespoons tamarind paste
6 kaffir lime (makrut) leaves, crushed
1½ tablespoons grated palm sugar (jaggery)
sea salt

rendang curry paste (makes about 400 g/14 oz)
15 g (½ oz) shrimp paste
1 red onion, roughly chopped
8 garlic cloves, chopped
12 long red chillies, seeds removed and chopped
1 lemon grass stem, white part only, chopped
40 g (1½ oz) galangal, peeled and finely chopped
40 g (1½ oz) ginger, peeled and finely chopped
finely grated zest of 1 kaffir lime (makrut)
5 g (⅛ oz) fresh turmeric, grated, or 1 teaspoon
    ground turmeric

Serves 4

To make the curry paste, first wrap the shrimp paste in foil and roast for about 10 minutes in a medium oven until fragrant. Blend or process all the ingredients together to form a smooth paste.

For the curry, heat the oil in a pan or wok. Add the curry paste and fry for 3 minutes — this will release a very strong chilli fragrance, but it is a necessary part of the recipe and will be well worth it. Add the beef, coconut milk, tamarind paste and kaffir lime leaves. Simmer, uncovered, stirring frequently (so the coconut milk doesn't stick) for 1–1½ hours, or until the meat is tender and the gravy has thickened. Add the palm sugar and salt to taste. Serve with steamed jasmine rice (page 244).

Grilled aged rib-eye with tomato and onion salsa This is not a minute steak; it is a 2-minute steak. The quality of the beef will reward you here. Make sure you cook on a really high heat — you want the outside to be caramelized and the interior melting.

4 x 250 g (9 oz) rib-eye steaks, beaten to 1 cm (1/2 inch) thick
sea salt
extra virgin olive oil
1 small piece horseradish, peeled
2 cm (3/4 inch) piece ginger, peeled
1 lemon

tomato and onion salsa
2 large vine-ripened tomatoes, peeled, seeds removed and finely diced (page 19)
1/2 red onion, finely diced
1 tablespoon roughly chopped flat-leaf (Italian) parsley
sea salt and freshly ground pepper
100 ml (31/2 fl oz) extra virgin olive oil
2 tablespoons red wine vinegar

Serves 4

Heat a flat or ridged grill-pan on top of the stove or heat the barbecue to very hot (you could also use a heavy-based pan). Season the steaks well with sea salt, up to 2 hours before cooking. Rub with some oil. Place the steaks on the heat, cook for 1 minute, then turn over and cook for a further minute, before removing from the heat. Allow to rest in a warm place for 5 minutes.

To make the salsa, simply mix the tomato, onion and parsley together with salt, pepper, oil and red wine vinegar to taste.

Place the steaks onto four serving plates, add the salsa and grate a little horseradish and ginger directly over the top. Finish with a squeeze of lemon juice.

Great with: I love a steak like this with chips (page 242) and a green salad, or boiled mixed greens.

Beef sirloin steak with tomato and leek sauce

This is one of the first sauces I made as a professional chef; it is delicious and simple and really complements crusty meat. The quantity below is too much for this dish alone, but it is worth making the full amount. Serve the leftover sauce with pasta or grilled (broiled) meats such as chicken or lamb.

4 x 250 g (9 oz) sirloin steaks
sea salt
extra virgin olive oil
freshly ground pepper

tomato and leek sauce
500 g (1 lb 2 oz) vine-ripened tomatoes, halved
sea salt and freshly ground pepper
50 ml (1½ fl oz) extra virgin olive oil
1 leek, thinly sliced
1 baby fennel bulb, thinly sliced
3 garlic cloves, finely chopped
125 ml (4 fl oz/½ cup) white wine
2 red capsicums (peppers), roasted, peeled and cut into 1 cm (½ inch) dice (page 176)
300 ml (10½ fl oz) chicken stock (page 245)
2 bay leaves, fresh if available
juice of 1 lemon

Serves 4

To make the tomato and leek sauce, place the tomato halves on a wire rack over a baking dish and season with a little sea salt and ground pepper. Roast for 1 hour and 40 minutes at 120°C (235°F/Gas ½), allow to cool, then remove from the rack and roughly chop.

Heat the oil in a large pan, add the leek, fennel, garlic and a pinch of sea salt and sweat over low heat for about 10 minutes until softened. Pour in the wine and allow it to reduce to a tablespoon. Stir in the roasted capsicum, chopped tomato, stock and bay leaves and simmer, covered, for 10 minutes. Remove the bay leaves, purée to a smooth consistency, then stir in the lemon juice and check the seasoning.

Season the steaks with some sea salt up to 2 hours before cooking, then drizzle with oil and place on a barbecue grill preheated to hot. Cook for 4 minutes, then turn over and cook for a further 4 minutes for rare (or a minute longer each side for medium–rare). Remove from the grill and allow to rest in a warm place for 10 minutes.

Place a spoonful of sauce on each of four plates. On a chopping board, slice the sirloins into four slices each and place on top of the sauce. Sprinkle some sea salt directly onto the meat and give a good grind of pepper, then serve.

Great with: Potato gratin (page 241) and broccoli.

Rump steak with porcini and roast garlic butter This is a dish where the steak needs to be cut thick and cooked rare. The porcini add great flavour to this butter — they are expensive, but you need very little to make a difference — and it is really worth roasting the garlic to get that nice caramel flavour.

4 x 250 g (9 oz) beef rump steaks
extra virgin olive oil
sea salt and freshly ground pepper

porcini and roast garlic butter
30 g (1 oz) dried porcini mushrooms
250 g (9 oz/1 cup) unsalted butter
1 head of garlic, roasted until soft, skin removed
juice of 1 lemon
2 tablespoons finely chopped flat-leaf (Italian) parsley
sea salt

Serves 4

To make the porcini and roast garlic butter, soak the porcini in boiling water for 30 minutes, or until soft. Drain and roughly chop. Put the porcini, butter, roasted garlic, lemon juice, parsley and salt in a food processor and process until all the ingredients are well combined.

Roll the butter mixture into a log shape, about 35 cm (14 inches) long and 4 cm (1½ inches) in diameter, and wrap in baking paper or plastic wrap, then refrigerate until needed. Just before cooking the rump, cut the butter into 1 cm (½ inch) thick rounds and remove the paper or plastic. Allow to come to room temperature and allow for about three slices of butter per person. Refrigerate or freeze any remaining butter for a later date and dish.

Drizzle the steaks with oil and sprinkle both sides with sea salt. Heat a grill (broiler) or barbecue to hot, place the steaks on and cook for 5 minutes. When a good crust forms, turn and cook for a further 4 minutes, then remove and rest in a warm place for 10 minutes.

Place the steaks on a board and cut each one into 5 mm (¼ inch) thick slices. Arrange on the plate and top with the porcini butter, sprinkle on some sea salt, give a good grind of pepper and serve.

Great with: Yam purée and a big bowl of steamed broccolini.

Barbecued beef fillet with horseradish crème fraîche This dish is breathtakingly simple and so delicious. This cream is good on all barbecued food, and any leftovers will keep for two days in the fridge. Be aware that different brands of prepared horseradish can vary greatly in strength, so taste as you go. You can of course just roast the fillet.

4 x 200 g (7 oz) prime beef fillet steaks
sea salt
extra virgin olive oil
juice of 1 lemon
freshly ground pepper

horseradish crème fraîche
60 g (2 1/4 oz/1/4 cup) crème fraîche
50 g (1 3/4 oz) prepared horseradish, or to taste
sea salt and freshly ground pepper
squeeze of lemon juice
50 ml (1 1/2 fl oz) cream (whipping)

Serves 4

Preheat the barbecue to hot. To make the horseradish crème fraîche, mix the crème fraîche and horseradish in a bowl until well combined, and season with sea salt, fresh pepper and lemon juice. In a bowl, lightly whip the cream and then fold through the crème fraîche mixture. Check the seasoning.

Season the steaks with sea salt up to 2 hours before cooking. Drizzle with oil and place onto the hot barbecue. Cook for 5 minutes, then turn over and cook for a further 5 minutes. Remove from the grill and allow to rest for 10 minutes in a warm place. Place a steak on each plate with a large spoonful of horseradish crème fraîche over the top and a squeeze of lemon, season with a little sea salt and give a good grind of fresh pepper. Serve.

Great with: Again, I love chips (page 242) with this, but potato purée (page 243) or potato gratin (page 241) would also be wonderful along with a bowl of boiled peas or snow peas (mangetout).

Beef fillet with carrot and yam tagine

I love this dish! We serve it on Qantas, where it gets the heart-smart tick of approval — so tasty and good for you. Make or buy some harissa, the fiery Moroccan condiment. It really kicks the whole thing along.

4 x 185 g (6¹/2 oz) beef fillets
extra virgin olive oil
harissa (page 245)
couscous (page 244)

chermoula paste
1 red onion, roughly chopped
4 garlic cloves, roughly chopped
¹/2 bunch flat-leaf (Italian) parsley, about 75 g (2¹/2 oz)
¹/2 bunch coriander (cilantro) leaves, about 40 g (1¹/2 oz)
juice of 1 lemon
1 tablespoon ground cumin
2 teaspoons sweet paprika
2 teaspoons ground turmeric
1 teaspoon ground chilli
125 ml (4 fl oz/¹/2 cup) extra virgin olive oil
sea salt

carrot and yam tagine
2 carrots, sliced into 2 cm (³/4 inch) thick rounds
1 large yam (or sweet potato), peeled and cut into 2 cm (³/4 inch) thick pieces
2 tablespoons extra virgin olive oil
8 baby onions, halved if large
1 teaspoon ground cinnamon
1 teaspoon ground ginger
1 tablespoon honey
110 g (3³/4 oz/¹/2 cup) pitted prunes
500 ml (17 fl oz/2 cups) chicken stock (page 245)
2 tablespoons coarsely chopped coriander (cilantro) leaves
2 tablespoons finely chopped mint

Serves 4

To make the chermoula, blend or process all the ingredients together to form a paste, then set aside. Marinate the beef fillets in the chermoula for about 1 hour.

For the tagine, heat the oil in a large, heavy-based saucepan over low–medium heat. Add the onion and cook, stirring occasionally, for 5–10 minutes, or until soft. Increase the heat to medium and add the carrot and yam. Cook, stirring occasionally, until they are lightly browned. Add the spices, honey and prunes and stir to combine. Stir in the chicken stock, bring to a simmer, cover and cook for 10–15 minutes, or until the vegetables are just tender. Remove the lid and simmer for a further 5–10 minutes, or until the sauce reduces and thickens. Stir through the coriander and mint.

Meanwhile, preheat the oven to 200°C (400°F/Gas 6). Heat a little oil in a heavy-based, ovenproof frying pan until very hot and sear the beef on all sides (don't worry if it looks a little burnt, it adds to the taste). Transfer the pan to the oven and cook the beef for 12 minutes, then remove and rest in a warm place for 10 minutes.

Divide the tagine among four large bowls and place a sliced beef fillet on top of each. Drizzle with a little harissa and serve with couscous.

T-bone steak, Italian-style There is no use mucking around with this one. Get the big daddy T-bone with a large piece of fillet. Get them cut thick and really enjoy what a good steak can taste like. Now, if you want to go the whole hog, do what I do: light a barbecue and smoke the meat with a little hickory or mesquite wood and you will be over the moon with the results. I love building a fire and cooking a steak over it, that is really barbecuing. Maybe it's the hunter coming out in me, I don't know, but I don't find it a chore; I find it a joy.

4 T-bone steaks
1 small handful oregano leaves
1 rosemary sprig, leaves picked
6 sage leaves
extra virgin olive oil
sea salt
4 garlic cloves, chopped
2 bunches English spinach, about 200 g (7 oz),
   trimmed and washed
freshly ground pepper
1 lemon

Serves 4

Roughly chop the herbs and press them on to both sides of the steak.

Heat a chargrill pan or barbecue until smoking. Drizzle the steaks with oil and season with sea salt. Grill them for about 6 minutes on one side, then 4 minutes on the other, or cook to your liking. Remove and place in a warm oven to rest for 10 minutes.

Heat a little oil in a non-stick pan. Add the garlic with a little salt and sweat well, without colouring. Add the spinach and cook until wilted. For a warm spinach salad, remove it from the pan at this point, or alternatively, leave it a little longer to braise down.

To serve, place the steaks onto four dinner plates and pour the juices over. Add a splash of oil and plenty of fresh pepper. Place the spinach beside the steaks and serve with lemon.

Slow-braised beef with artichokes and pine nuts

This is a delicious braise, but as with all braises, take your time and simmer it very slowly; that is the secret to meltingly tender meat.

800 g (1 lb 12 oz) beef chuck, cut into 3 cm (1¼ inch) dice
3 tablespoons extra virgin olive oil
1 small onion, sliced
4 garlic cloves, cut into thin slices
3 cm (1¼ inch) piece ginger, peeled and grated
sea salt
1 teaspoon ground cumin
500 ml (17 fl oz/2 cups) dry red wine
3 tablespoons balsamic vinegar
800 ml (28 fl oz) beef stock
8 preserved artichoke hearts, quartered lengthways
2 tablespoons pine nuts, lightly roasted
2 tablespoons roughly chopped flat-leaf (Italian) parsley
juice of 1 lemon

Serves 4

Heat the oil in a large pan and brown the beef on all sides — you will need to do this in batches. Remove the beef from the pan and set aside. Add the onion, garlic, ginger and some sea salt to the pan and sauté until golden. Add the cumin and cook for a further minute, then add the wine and vinegar and simmer until reduced to about 125 ml (4 fl oz/½ cup). Return the beef to the pan, add the stock and bring to the boil. Reduce the heat to low, cover and cook for about 1 hour and 20 minutes — the beef should be meltingly tender by this stage.

Use a slotted spoon to remove the beef from the pan. Increase the heat and simmer the sauce until it reduces and thickens. Gently fold the beef, artichokes, pine nuts, parsley and lemon juice through the sauce. Taste and adjust the seasoning if necessary.

Great with: Crusty bread or mashed potato.

Slow-roast beef with braised peas and yorkshire puddings
This is the most incredible Sunday lunch, especially with béarnaise rather than gravy. Note that the oil or duck fat for the puddings must be smoking hot so the batter becomes light and puffed up as soon as it hits the hot oil.

3-bone rib of beef, about 1.25 kg (2 lb 12 oz)
sea salt
extra virgin olive oil
braised peas (page 240)
béarnaise (page 247)

yorkshire puddings
150 g (5¹/2 oz/1 heaped cup) plain (all-purpose) flour
¹/2 teaspoon sea salt
2 eggs
125 ml (4 fl oz/¹/2 cup) milk
170 ml (5¹/2 fl oz/²/3 cup) vegetable oil or duck fat

Serves 4

First make the batter for the yorkshire puddings. It is best to do this a couple of hours ahead of time, if possible (even the day before, if time permits), and allow it to rest. Simply sift the flour and salt into a large bowl and whisk in the combined eggs, milk and 125 ml (4 fl oz/¹/2 cup) water until smooth. Cover and set aside to rest (in the refrigerator, if overnight).

Remove the beef from the refrigerator a couple of hours before you intend to cook it, season it well with sea salt and let it come to room temperature. Preheat the oven to 70°C (150°F/Gas ¹/4), or as low as it will go (check the temperature with an oven thermometer). Rub the rib with oil and put it in a roasting tin. Put the tin in the oven and turn it every 30 minutes or so, to ensure even cooking. About 1¹/2 hours into the roasting time, slide the meat thermometer into the centre of the beef to check the core cooking temperature. Remove the thermometer and continue to cook until the reading is 53°C (127°F). This can take 4 hours or even longer. If your oven is a little hotter, take the meat out 1–2 degrees earlier.

When the beef has reached the desired temperature, take it out of the oven, remove it from the tin and wrap it in a double layer of foil, then in a tea towel (dish towel) — you want the meat to retain its heat while it rests. Rest the beef in a warm place for 30 minutes. Unwrap the rested beef and use a sharp knife to remove the bones. Heat a large frying pan with a healthy splash of oil until the oil is just below smoking. Add the beef to the pan and sear it well on all sides until the entire rib has a lovely crust.

Meanwhile, heat the oven to 240°C (475°F/Gas 8). Divide the vegetable oil or duck fat among 8 holes of a 12-cup muffin tin. Put the tin on the highest shelf of the oven and allow it to heat for 5–10 minutes until the oil is smoking. Working quickly but carefully, remove the hot tin from the oven and pour the batter evenly among the oiled holes — the batter will bubble and start to puff up immediately. Quickly return the tin to the top shelf of the oven and cook for 15 minutes, or until the puddings are golden. Remove the puddings from the oven and transfer them to a wire rack, so they don't go soggy in the tin.

To serve, place the beef on a board and slice it into four rounds. Place each round in the centre of four large shallow bowls. Spoon some braised peas over, add some béarnaise sauce and place a warm pudding next to it. Serve immediately.

Carrot and almond cake

This gorgeous cake is simple to make and perfect for a Sunday afternoon tea, or to take on a picnic.

185 g (6½ oz/1¾ cups) ground almonds
100 g (3½ oz/1 cup) walnuts, lightly roasted
230 g (8 oz/1 cup) caster (superfine) sugar
125 g (4½ oz) savoiardi (lady finger) biscuits,
    roughly chopped
2½ teaspoons baking powder
5 eggs, separated
1 large carrot, finely grated
1 tablespoon Grand Marnier
finely grated zest of 1 orange
icing (confectioners') sugar, for dusting
thick (double/heavy) cream

Serves 8

Lightly grease a 23 cm (9 inch) round cake tin and line the base and sides with baking paper.

Place the almonds, walnuts and sugar in a food processor and process to form coarse crumbs. Transfer the crumb mixture to a large mixing bowl. Process the savoiardi biscuits and baking powder together until the biscuits are finely crushed, then combine them with the crumb mixture. Add the lightly beaten egg yolks, carrot, Grand Marnier and orange zest to the crumb mixture, and mix until all the ingredients are moistened and well combined.

Preheat the oven to 180°C (350°F/Gas 4). Beat the egg whites until firm peaks form. Gently fold the egg whites into the cake mixture in three batches. Spoon the mixture into the prepared tin and bake for about 40 minutes, or until cooked when tested with a skewer. Transfer the cake to a wire rack to cool. Dust with icing sugar, cut into wedges and serve with cream. Serve warm or at room temperature.

White forest cake

This is an absolute cracker. Easy to make and it looks fabulous all white. There is something really alluring about fresh cake and cream — it takes me back to my childhood, when the local cake shop made all their cakes that way. Those days have long passed, sadly. Don't look at this recipe and say 'This is too long for me'. It involves just making a cake, stewing some fruit and whipping cream. It started out life as a quick version of Black Forest Cake, but once you have perfection, why add more cherries and lots of chocolate? Good cooking is all about knowing when to stop. You'll love where we have stopped.

cherries in brandy
750 g (1 lb 10 oz) fresh cherries, pitted
250 ml (9 fl oz/1 cup) brandy
2 tablespoons caster (superfine) sugar

cake
225 g (8 oz) unsalted butter, softened
225 g (8 oz/1 cup) caster (superfine) sugar
1 teaspoon natural vanilla extract
1/2 teaspoon natural almond extract
9 eggs, separated
250 g (9 oz) dark (semisweet) chocolate, coarsely
   grated
125 g (4 1/2 oz/1 cup) plain (all-purpose) flour, sifted
3 teaspoons baking powder
pinch of salt
100 g (3 1/2 oz/1 cup) ground almonds

filling
180 ml (8 fl oz/3/4 cup) kirsch
375 ml (13 fl oz/1 1/2 cups) cream (whipping),
   whipped to stiff peaks

icing
750 ml (26 fl oz/3 cups) cream (whipping)
125 g (4 1/2 oz/1 cup) icing (confectioners') sugar,
   sifted

Serves 8

To make the cherries in brandy, put the brandy and sugar in a pan over low heat and stir continuously, until the sugar has dissolved. Increase the heat and bring the mixture to the boil. Add the cherries, reduce the heat to low and simmer, covered, for about 10 minutes, or until the cherries are quite tender, but still holding their shape. Remove the cherries from the liquid using a slotted spoon, and set them aside. Increase the heat to medium and simmer the liquid for 5–10 minutes, or until almost all the liquid has evaporated and you have a syrup (be sure to watch the syrup towards the end of the cooking time so it doesn't burn). Toss the syrup with the cherries and set aside to cool completely.

Meanwhile, to make the cake, preheat the oven to 160°C (315°F/Gas 2–3). Grease three 23 cm (9 inch) round cake tins, and line the bases and sides with baking paper. Put the butter, 170 g (6 oz/3/4 cup) of the sugar and the vanilla and almond extracts into a large bowl and beat with an electric mixer until light and fluffy. Reduce the speed to low and gradually add the egg yolks, beating until incorporated. Fold in the combined chocolate, flour, baking powder, salt and ground almonds. Beat the egg whites in a bowl with an electric mixer until frothy. Add the remaining sugar and beat to stiff peaks. Fold the egg whites into the cake mixture in three or four batches. Divide the batter evenly among the prepared cake tins, and smooth out the surfaces with a spatula.

Bake the cakes for 20 minutes, or until cooked when tested with a skewer. Allow the cakes to cool briefly, then turn out onto wire racks lined with baking paper. Cool completely.

To assemble, place one cake upside down on a cake plate. Drizzle with one-third of the kirsch, then spread with half the cream and sprinkle with half the cherries. Place another cake on top and repeat the process. Place the last cake on top, and drizzle with the remaining kirsch. For the icing, whip the cream and sugar together until soft peaks form, then frost the top and sides of the cake. You now have a big beautiful white cake. Yum!

Lemon yoghurt cake with peach and blueberry salad

This cake is inspired by the wonderful cookbook writer Claudia Roden. Her Middle Eastern books are so fabulous; I recommend them to anyone who loves Moroccan, Turkish, Lebanese, Egyptian or Jewish cooking. Simple and delicious, this cake can be enjoyed with a little whipped cream or with any fruit combination that is in season. Here I have suggested a peach and blueberry salad. Don't expect this to be light; it has the texture of a heavy cheesecake, but is oh so heavenly.

4 large eggs, separated
100 g (3½ oz/heaped ⅓ cup) caster (superfine) sugar
3 tablespoons plain (all-purpose) flour
400 g (14 oz/1¾ cups) Greek-style yoghurt
grated zest of 1 lemon
juice of 1 lemon
icing (confectioners') sugar, for dusting
whipped cream

peach and blueberry salad
6 ripe peaches, cut into wedges
155 g (5½ oz/1 cup) blueberries
55 g (2 oz/¼ cup) caster (superfine) sugar
grated zest of 1 lemon
juice of 1 lemon
1 vanilla bean

Serves 6

Preheat the oven to 180°C (350°F/Gas 4). Grease a 22 cm (8½ inch) spring-form cake tin with butter and line the base and side with baking paper. Beat the egg yolks with the sugar to a thick, pale cream. Beat in the flour, then the yoghurt, lemon zest and lemon juice until it is thoroughly blended. Whisk the egg whites until stiff and fold them into the yoghurt mixture in two batches. Pour the mixture into the prepared tin and bake for 50 minutes, or until cooked when tested with a skewer. Check the cake after 30 minutes, and cover with foil if over browning. Unclip the spring-form tin and slide the cake onto a wire rack to cool.

Meanwhile place the peaches, blueberries, sugar, lemon zest and lemon juice in a bowl. Split the vanilla bean lengthways and scrape out the seeds. Add these to the fruit salad and toss all the ingredients until combined. Cover the bowl and set aside at room temperature to macerate for several hours.

Transfer the cake to a serving plate and dust with icing sugar. Serve wedges of cake with peach and blueberry salad and a dollop of whipped cream.

Olive oil and sauternes cake with roast pears I first cooked an olive oil cake out of the *Chez Panisse* pastry book and have loved making them ever since. Mind you, anything I cook out of any of the many *Chez Panisse* cookbooks always ends up my favourite. What else would you expect from one of the world's great restaurants? We have paired this one with pears, and a wonderful match it is. You could, however, just serve it with a little whipped cream, and it would be more than satisfying.

roast pears

4 beurre bosc pears, halved or quartered lengthways,
   core removed, stem intact
80 ml (2^{1}/$_{2}$ fl oz/^{1}/$_{3}$ cup) sauternes dessert wine
2 tablespoons olive oil
2 tablespoons caster (superfine) sugar

cake

115 g (4 oz/^{1}/$_{2}$ cup) caster (superfine) sugar
2 eggs
185 ml (6 fl oz/^{3}/$_{4}$ cup) olive oil
125 ml (4 fl oz/^{1}/$_{2}$ cup) sauternes dessert wine
80 ml (2^{1}/$_{2}$ fl oz/^{1}/$_{3}$ cup) milk
finely grated zest of 2 lemons
185 g (6^{1}/$_{2}$ oz/1^{1}/$_{2}$ cups) plain (all-purpose) flour
2^{1}/$_{2}$ teaspoons baking powder

sauternes syrup

115 g (4 oz/^{1}/$_{2}$ cup) caster (superfine) sugar
125 ml (4 fl oz/^{1}/$_{2}$ cup) sauternes dessert wine

thick (double/heavy) cream

Serves 8

Preheat the oven to 180°C (350°F/Gas 4). Place the pears in a roasting tin, drizzle with the wine and oil and sprinkle with the sugar. Roast for 45 minutes, turning occasionally, until tender and starting to caramelize. Allow to cool to room temperature.

Meanwhile, to make the cake, lightly grease an 11 x 22 cm (4^{1}/$_{4}$ x 8 ^{1}/$_{2}$ inch) loaf (bar) tin, and line the base and sides with baking paper. Beat the sugar and eggs together in a large bowl with an electric mixer until pale and creamy. Add the oil, wine, milk and lemon zest and beat until well combined. Add the combined, sifted flour and baking powder and slowly beat until just combined. Pour the mixture into the prepared tin. Bake alongside the pears for 40 minutes, or until cooked when tested with a skewer. Allow to stand for 5 minutes before turning out onto a wire rack to cool completely.

Meanwhile, to make the sauternes syrup, place the sugar and 2 tablespoons water in a small pan and stir constantly, over very low heat, without letting it boil, until the sugar has completely dissolved. Increase the heat and allow the syrup to simmer, brushing the side of the pan with a wet pastry brush if necessary, until the syrup turns a golden colour. It is important to keep an eye on the syrup at all times, as once it starts to colour, it will continue to darken very quickly. Turn off the heat, add the wine and stir to combine. Some of the syrup may solidify at this point. If this is the case, return it to a very low heat until it dissolves again. Set aside to cool.

Serve the cake with the pears, drizzle with the syrup and add a dollop of cream.

Baked pear clafoutis The classic clafoutis is, of course, cherry, but this batter works well with any fruit. Many clafoutis recipes always turn out too heavy to me, but this one is inspired from a recipe in Michel Roux' wonderful book *Eggs*, a must for every home. He is an amazing chef, but an even better communicator on all things to do with food.

batter

2 eggs

60 g (2¼ oz/½ cup) plain (all-purpose) flour

80 g (2⅔ oz/⅓ cup) caster (superfine) sugar, plus extra, to dust

½ vanilla bean, split lengthways and seeds scraped

80 g (2⅔ oz/scant ⅓ cup) unsalted butter, melted and cooled

170 ml (5½ fl oz/⅔ cup) cold milk

1 tablespoon Poire William (optional)

baked pears

3–4 beurre bosc pears (the number of pears will depend on the size of the dish)

1 tablespoon unsalted butter

1 tablespoon caster (superfine) sugar

60 g (2¼ oz/¼ cup) unsalted butter, diced

Serves 6–8

For the baked pears, preheat the oven to 220°C (425°F/Gas 7). Halve the pears lengthways, leaving the stalks intact, and remove the cores with a melon baller or paring knife. Melt the butter in a large, heavy-based, ovenproof frying pan over medium heat and sprinkle with the sugar. Arrange the pear halves cut side down, over the sugar, and cook undisturbed for 3–5 minutes, or until the sugar begins to caramelize. Transfer the frying pan to the oven and bake the pears for about 20–25 minutes, or until tender. Lower the oven temperature to 200°C (400°F/Gas 6).

Generously grease the base and sides of a 2.5–3 litre (87–105 fl oz/10–12 cup) baking dish with a little of the diced butter. Place the pears, cut side up, over the base of the dish and pour over the syrup. Set aside to cool.

To make the batter, put the eggs, flour, sugar and vanilla seeds in a bowl and whisk until smooth. Gradually whisk in the cooled melted butter, the milk and the Poire William, if using. Pour the batter over the pears and bake for 10 minutes. Remove the dish from the oven, lower the temperature to 180°C (350°F/Gas 4) and scatter the remaining diced butter over the top of the clafoutis. Return the dish to the oven for a further 20–25 minutes, or until puffed and golden.

To check if the clafoutis is cooked, slide in a knife tip or skewer; if it comes out clean and easily, it is ready. Dust with a little caster sugar and leave to stand for a few minutes before serving.

Sticky toffee pudding

The classic sticky date pudding! This is everything you expect and more. Incredibly rich and full on — but if you can handle it, you will be hooked forever.

10 fresh dates, about 230 g (8 oz), pitted and chopped
1 teaspoon bicarbonate of soda (baking soda)
100 g (3^1/$_2$ oz/^{1}/$_3$ cup) unsalted butter, softened
175 g (6 oz/^{3}/$_4$ cup) caster (superfine) sugar
2 eggs
1 teaspoon natural vanilla extract
150 g (5^1/$_2$ oz/1^1/$_4$ cups) self-raising flour, sifted
thick (double/heavy) cream

sauce
500 ml (17 fl oz/2 cups) thick (double/heavy) cream
110 g (3^3/$_4$ oz/^{1}/$_2$ cup) demerara sugar
2 tablespoons treacle or molasses

Serves 8

Preheat the oven to 180°C (350°F/Gas 4). Grease a 27 x 15 x 6 cm (10^3/$_4$ x 6 x 2^1/$_2$ inch) deep loaf (bar) tin and line the base and sides with baking paper. Place the dates and 250 ml (9 fl oz/1 cup) water into a pan and bring to the boil over medium heat. Remove the pan from the heat and add the bicarbonate of soda — the mixture will begin to bubble up. Set aside to cool.

Meanwhile, use an electric mixer to cream the butter and sugar together until light and fluffy. Add the eggs, one at a time, beating after each addition. Add the vanilla and beat until combined. Fold the flour and the date mixture alternately into the butter mixture. Pour the batter into the prepared tin, and bake for 50 minutes, or until cooked when tested with a skewer.

To make the sauce, combine the cream, sugar and treacle in a small pan and stir constantly over medium heat until the sugar has dissolved. Bring the mixture to the boil, then reduce to a simmer, stirring occasionally, until the sauce reduces and thickens slightly.

To serve, turn the warm pudding out onto a platter and drizzle with half the sauce. Cut the pudding into thick slices or squares and serve with the remaining sauce and thick cream. If the pudding needs to be reheated, cover it with foil and place it in a 150°C (300°F/Gas 2) oven for 30 minutes, or until heated through.

Summer berry parfait Parfaits are simple because you don't need an ice-cream machine, so you can have a frozen dessert with minimal fuss. Feel free to use frozen berries when fresh are out of season or just too expensive.

coulis
300 g (10½ oz) raspberries
100 ml (3½ fl oz) sugar syrup (see Note)

raspberry parfait
150 g (5½ oz) raspberries
2 tablespoons sugar syrup
80 ml (2½ fl oz/⅓ cup) milk
55 g (2 oz/¼ cup) caster (superfine) sugar
3 egg yolks
170 ml (5½ fl oz/⅔ cup) cream (whipping)

vanilla parfait
80 ml (2½ fl oz/⅓ cup) milk, with ¼ vanilla bean,
    scraped and infused in the milk
55 g (2 oz/¼ cup) caster (superfine) sugar
3 egg yolks
170 ml (5½ fl oz/⅔ cup) cream (whipping)

strawberry parfait
250 g (9 oz) strawberries
2 tablespoons sugar syrup
80 ml (2½ fl oz/⅓ cup) milk
55 g (2 oz/¼ cup) caster (superfine) sugar
3 egg yolks
170 ml (5½ fl oz/⅔ cup) cream (whipping)

assorted fresh berries
icing (confectioners') sugar (optional)

Serves 8

To make the coulis, simply blend the berries with the sugar syrup, strain and set aside.

To make the raspberry parfait, blend the raspberries with the sugar syrup and strain. Whisk the milk, sugar and egg yolks together in a bowl over boiling water, until the temperature when tested with a pastry thermometer reaches 84°C (183°F). Place the bowl over ice to cool completely. Whip the cream until soft peaks form, then gently fold the cream, followed by the raspberry syrup mixture, into the egg yolk mixture. Divide the parfait mixture among eight 200 ml (7 fl oz) serving glasses. Place the glasses on a tray and freeze.

When the raspberry parfait is completely frozen, you can start with the vanilla. Use the same method as for the raspberry, omitting the puréed berries and sugar syrup, and discarding the vanilla bean before adding the milk. Pour the vanilla parfait over the top of the frozen raspberry parfait, and freeze as before.

When the vanilla parfait is frozen, make the strawberry parfait using exactly the same method as for the raspberry parfait. Pour the strawberry parfait over the vanilla layer and freeze (there should be about 5 mm (¼ inch) of space left at the top of each glass). When ready to serve, remove the parfaits from the freezer, drizzle with coulis, sprinkle with berries and dust with icing sugar, if desired.

Note: Sugar syrup is made simply by bringing 2 parts water to 1 part caster (superfine) sugar to the boil together. Simmer until the sugar has completely dissolved, and set aside to cool.

Mango and passionfruit trifle

Here is another dessert that looks great in a glass. To make it easier, these trifles can also be poured into a tray or bowl and set, and then just scooped onto a plate.

2 small mangoes, cut into 1 cm (1/2 inch) dice
80 ml (2 1/2 fl oz/1/3 cup) Grand Marnier
300 ml (10 1/2 fl oz) cream (whipping), whipped to firm peaks

orange cake
100 g (3 1/2 oz/1/3 cup) unsalted butter, softened
185 g (6 1/2 oz/heaped 3/4 cup) caster (superfine) sugar
finely grated zest of 1 orange
2 eggs, separated
185 g (6 1/2 oz/1 1/2 cups) self-raising flour
125 ml (4 fl oz/1/2 cup) fresh orange juice
55 g (2 oz/1/4 cup) caster (superfine) sugar, extra

passionfruit curd
4 eggs
6 egg yolks
250 g (9 oz/heaped 1 cup) caster (superfine) sugar
250 ml (9 fl oz/1 cup) passionfruit juice (you will need to sieve the pulp from about 12 large passionfruit)

jelly
180 g (6 1/2 oz/3/4 cup) caster (superfine) sugar
750 ml (26 fl oz/3 cups) passionfruit juice (using the pulp from about 24 large passionfruit)
170 ml (5 1/2 fl oz/2/3 cup) lime juice
6 x 30 g (1 oz) gelatine leaves

Makes 8

To make the orange cake, preheat the oven to 180°C (350°F/Gas 4). Line a 20 x 30 cm (8 x 12 inch) shallow baking tin with baking paper, extending the paper 5 cm (2 inches) above the edges of the tin. Beat the butter, sugar and orange zest in a large bowl with an electric mixer until pale and creamy. Add the egg yolks, one at a time, beating well between each addition. Fold in the sifted flour alternately with the orange juice, until well combined. In a separate bowl, beat the egg whites until soft peaks form, then gradually add the extra sugar; beat until the sugar has dissolved. Fold the egg whites into the cake mixture in two or three batches. Spread the mixture into the prepared tin and bake for 20 minutes, or until cooked when tested with a skewer. Allow the cake to cool before cutting into 1 cm (1/2 inch) cubes.

To make the passionfruit curd, whisk the whole eggs, yolks, sugar and juice together in a large heat-proof bowl until well combined. Place the bowl over a pan of gently simmering water (there only needs to be about 5 cm (2 inches) of water in the base of the pan, and it should not come into contact with the base of the bowl). Whisk constantly until the curd thickens, for about 8 minutes. Remove from the heat and pass through a fine sieve; refrigerate until cool.

To make the jelly, combine the sugar, passionfruit and lime juice in a small saucepan. Place over medium heat and stir until the sugar has dissolved and the mixture comes almost to the boil. Remove from the heat. Place the gelatine leaves in a bowl of cold water to soften. Remove the gelatine from the water and add to the passionfruit mixture; mix until the gelatine has completely dissolved. Pour the jelly through a sieve into a large bowl. Discard the seeds and refrigerate the jelly until almost set — this will take about 45 minutes.

To assemble the trifles, divide the mango among eight 400 ml (14 fl oz) glasses or one 3.2 litre (112 fl oz) dish. Layer the cake over the mango and drizzle with Grand Marnier. Spoon the curd over the cake, then spread the cream evenly over the curd — you want a flat surface. Refrigerate the trifles for about 20 minutes, or until the cream is firm. Pour the jelly evenly over the cream and then refrigerate until the jelly is set.

Lemon tart

Lemon tart is one of the classic French desserts; every restaurant in Sydney seemed to have one on the menu during the 1980s and 90s. The reason is simple — they are so good! This is a really easy one, so dive in and enjoy.

pastry
150 g (5¹/2 oz/1¹/4 cups) plain (all-purpose) flour
40 g (1¹/2 oz/¹/3 cup) icing (confectioners') sugar
pinch of salt
40 g (1¹/4 oz) cold unsalted butter, chopped
1 egg yolk
1¹/2 tablespoons milk

filling
3 eggs
165 g (5³/4 oz/³/4 cup) caster (superfine) sugar
150 ml (5 fl oz) lemon juice
1¹/2 tablespoons plain (all-purpose) flour

softly whipped cream

Serves 8

To make the pastry, process the flour, sugar, salt and butter together until combined. Add the egg yolk and milk and pulse until the mixture just comes together. Turn the dough onto a lightly floured surface and knead lightly. Press the dough into a disc shape, wrap in plastic wrap and refrigerate for about 45 minutes. Remove the pastry from the fridge, and roll into a circle large enough to line a 22 cm (8¹/2 inch) fluted, loose-based tart tin. Ease the pastry into the tin, trim the edge, and prick the base all over with a fork. Refrigerate for a further 30 minutes.

Preheat the oven to 180°C (350°F/Gas 4). Line the pastry with foil and fill with uncooked rice, dried beans or pastry weights. Bake for 15 minutes. Carefully remove the foil and weights and return to the oven for a further 10 minutes, or until crisp and lightly golden. Allow to cool.

For the filling, beat the eggs and sugar together with electric beaters until thick and creamy. Gradually add the lemon juice, then the flour, and mix until just combined. Pour the filling into the pastry shell and bake at 180°C (350°F/Gas 4) for 15 minutes — the top will be well browned. Reduce the oven temperature to 150°C (300°F/Gas 2) and bake for a further 10 minutes, or until the filling has set. Remove from the oven to cool. Serve slices of tart with softly whipped cream.

Rhubarb and mascarpone cream trifles This dessert is simple and very elegant; serve it in really beautiful glasses for the best effect. You can also set it in a large glass bowl and take it to the table to serve. The mascarpone cream is essentially the filling for tiramisu, so it is light and can be used with any fruit. You can throw in savoiardi soaked in the matching flavour of your fruit to make any trifle you like. Try peach, cherry, raspberry, stewed apple or pear … whichever way you go, you will make this over and over again, it is so beautiful. To make it even simpler, forget the pistachio brittle and top with roasted slivered almonds.

1 bunch rhubarb, about 500 g (1 lb 2 oz), trimmed and washed
100 g (3½ oz/heaped ⅓ cup) caster (superfine) sugar
juice of 1 lemon
125 g (4½ oz/¾ cup) strawberries, hulled and sliced
4 large savoiardi (lady fingers), chopped into 1 cm (½ inch) thick pieces

pistachio brittle
60 g (2¼ oz/heaped ⅓ cup) raw unsalted shelled pistachios
100 g (3½ oz/heaped ⅓ cup) caster (superfine) sugar

mascarpone cream
3 eggs, separated
80 g (2¾ oz/⅓ cup) caster (superfine) sugar
½ teaspoon natural vanilla extract
300 g (10½ oz/1⅓ cups) mascarpone

Serves 4

Preheat the oven to 100°C (200°F/Gas ½). Cut the rhubarb into 5 cm (2 inch) lengths and toss it with the sugar and lemon juice. Place the rhubarb mixture in a baking dish and cover tightly with foil. Bake for about 30 minutes, stirring occasionally, until very tender. Add the strawberries for the last 5 minutes of cooking time. Remove from the oven and set aside to cool.

To make the brittle, place the pistachios on a baking tray and bake at 180°C (350°F/Gas 4) for 5 minutes, or until golden. Remove from the oven and allow to cool. Combine the sugar and 3 tablespoons water in a small saucepan and stir over low heat until the sugar dissolves. Increase the heat to a boil, occasionally brushing the side of the pan with a wet pastry brush, until the syrup is golden in colour. Remove from the heat, allow the bubbles to subside, then drizzle over the nuts and leave to set until hard. Roughly chop the brittle into 1 cm (½ inch) thick pieces.

For the mascarpone cream, beat the egg yolks, 2 tablespoons of the sugar and the vanilla together until thick and pale. Add the mascarpone and whisk until smooth. Beat the egg whites until soft peaks start to form. Gradually add the remaining sugar, and beat until the sugar has dissolved. Fold the egg whites into the mascarpone mixture in three batches.

To assemble, divide the savoiardi biscuits among four 350 ml (12 fl oz) dessert glasses, or one large glass bowl. Spoon the rhubarb mixture evenly over the biscuits, then top with the mascarpone cream. Cover the glasses with plastic wrap and refrigerate for several hours, or until needed. Sprinkle the trifles with pistachio brittle just before serving.

Chocolate pots de crème
This is an elegant, but simple chocolate dessert that I first cooked with my great friend Damien Pignolet. Buy good-quality chocolate, as it really has a big effect on the end result.

125 ml (4 fl oz/½ cup) cream
125 ml (4 fl oz/½ cup) milk
75 g (2½ oz) good-quality dark chocolate buttons
3 egg yolks
2 tablespoons caster (superfine) sugar
1 teaspoon natural vanilla extract
thick (double/heavy) cream
good-quality cocoa, for dusting

Makes 4

Place the cream and milk in small heavy-based saucepan over medium heat. Bring the mixture almost to the boil, remove from the heat, then add the chocolate buttons and stir until the chocolate has completely melted.

Preheat the oven to 170°C (325°F/Gas 3). Whisk the egg yolks, sugar and vanilla together in a bowl. Add a little of the hot chocolate mixture to the eggs and whisk, then add the remaining chocolate mixture and whisk again until well combined. Strain the mixture through a fine sieve into a heatproof jug, and then pour evenly among four coffee cups. Place the cups in a small roasting tin and pour enough boiling water into the tin to come halfway up the sides of the coffee cups. Place the tin in the lower third of the oven and bake for 25 minutes, or until just set. Remove from the oven and place the cups on a wire rack to cool. Transfer the cups to the fridge to chill before serving with a dollop of cream and a dusting of cocoa.

Dark chocolate mousse If you love chocolate, it doesn't get any easier and certainly not any tastier than this. Choose a sexy glass and you will have a very sophisticated, no-fuss dessert indeed. Make the effort to get good-quality bitter chocolate — it is really worth it.

250 g (9 oz) good-quality dark chocolate, chopped
300 ml (10½ fl oz) thick (double/heavy) cream
1 strong espresso coffee, very short
3 extra large eggs, separated
150 ml (5 fl oz) cream (whipping), lightly whipped
50 g (1¾ oz) chocolate-coated coffee beans,
　　lightly crushed

Serves 4

Place the chocolate and cream in a stainless steel bowl on top of a saucepan of simmering water. Make sure the bowl fits snuggly into the saucepan; at the same time the bowl should not touch the water. You want just a gentle steam, so keep the heat very low. Stir frequently (the cream may look slightly split, but should come back together once it combines with the chocolate) until the chocolate and cream have melted and combined well. Remove the bowl from the pan and set aside to cool. Whisk the coffee and egg yolks into the chocolate mixture.

Beat the egg whites until stiff peaks form and then use a large metal spoon to fold the whites into the chocolate mixture in three batches.

Divide the mousse evenly among four glasses, cover with plastic wrap, and refrigerate for several hours or until firm. Remove the mousse from the fridge about 10 minutes before serving, top with whipped cream and sprinkle with chocolate-coated coffee beans.

There is a lot of debate about schools and their role in helping children to grow up with a healthy diet, and an understanding about food that will help them live happier, healthier adult lives. Yes, it is true that there should be healthy choices at school for our children, but taking soft drinks and chips out of schools won't solve the problem. It is through us and the example we set them that they learn how to live their lives. The responsibilty ends with us, the parents. Teach children that cooking is fun, show them how to eat and prepare fresh food, and help them to understand good taste. Fresh, not fast, food and a good amount of fun exercise are the way to a healthy, happy life.

Boiling and steaming vegetables

Boiling and steaming are both very pure ways of cooking vegetables. Most green and root vegetables can be cooked successfully by either method. Steaming is so easy, all you need is a saucepan of boiling water and a bamboo or other steamer basket. Make sure you don't boil the pan dry and don't burn yourself with the steam; other than that, you are away. You may find that when steaming you lose a little colour from green vegetables, though you will lose fewer nutrients than if boiling. Steaming will also take a little longer than boiling, maybe up to a third longer. That said, I do, for the most part, prefer boiled vegetables over steamed. There is an argument that says that salt is added to water only to increase the boiling temperature and that it has no effect on the taste. I have always disagreed with that. I find salted vegetables taste better, no matter what the scientists say.

When boiling, I will generally boil the vegetables, drain well and toss with extra virgin olive oil, sea salt and freshly ground pepper. It is then that you experience the true flavour of the vegetable. So when you pick fresh, in-season vegetables for this process you will get real flavour.

There are just a few things to remember when boiling vegetables: have fiercely boiling water; add to it a considerable amount of sea salt (it should taste like the sea); and don't cover green vegetables as that can make them lose their colour.

Cook vegetables to your liking by checking them as they are cooking: remove a pea or bean and have a munch. When you like what you taste, quickly remove them from the saucepan by draining them into a colander or fishing them out with a steel mesh strainer such as a spider; whichever option you follow, make sure you're ready and you move quickly.

My favourite vegetables to boil

Asparagus: The spears take 3–5 minutes depending on their thickness.

Broccoli: This vegetable takes about 5 minutes, and the flavour will really intensify if you cook it for the full amount of time.

Broccolini: A wonderful vegetable, with so many nutrients. Will only take about 4 minutes.

Brussels sprouts: If cooked whole, they will take about 8 minutes, but I quite often cut them in half and they will cook in no time. Great with butter.

Corn on the cob: Corn needs about 6–8 minutes. You can take the corn off the cob and serve, or roll the whole cob in a little butter and olive oil.

English spinach: An easy 1¹/₂ minutes, if that.

Green beans: They will take about 7–8 minutes. Don't forget that you want to cook beans for long enough to convert the starch to sugar to achieve really sweet-tasting beans.

Peas: About 3 minutes is enough for young peas.

Root vegetables: This includes yams, parsnips, carrots, celeriac and squash such as pumpkin. I like to boil these vegetables in just enough water so that the water is almost completely reduced by the time the vegetables are cooked. To do this, I don't completely cover the vegetables with water, but have the water level at about three-quarters of the height of the vegetables. I add some butter and sea salt and boil; the exposed parts will cook in the steam. Then I season, drizzle with extra virgin olive oil and serve. Quite often the vegetables will be breaking up when ready, but don't worry, as they are almost self-saucing and incredibly delicious. Follow this method when making purées, as the little bit of water left over at the end is full of great flavour and nutrients and can be incorporated into the purée. Treat yourself to a new toy and invest in a small stick blender for home. These are invaluable when it comes to puréeing vegetables (though not potatoes — too much starch) and equally great for quick marinades and dressings.

Snow peas (mangetout): They will only take about 2 minutes.

Sugar snap peas: They will take about 2–3 minutes.

Note: All of these vegetables work just brilliantly on a barbecue as well … a splash of extra virgin olive oil, season with sea salt and freshly ground pepper and away you go.

Braised peas

300 g (10½ oz/2 cups) freshly shelled peas, about
    700 g (1 lb 9 oz) unshelled
2 tablespoons extra virgin olive oil, plus extra,
    to serve
30 g (1 oz) unsalted butter, diced
8 anchovies, chopped
sea salt
freshly ground pepper
juice of ½ lemon

Serves 4

Heat the oil and butter together in a frying pan. Add the anchovies with a pinch of sea salt and allow the anchovies to melt in. Add the peas, toss well to coat, then add 400 ml (14 fl oz) water and leave until the liquid is reduced and the peas are soft. This will take at least 20 minutes. The peas need to be melting and sweet and the bright green colour a distant memory. Finish with a grind of pepper, a splash of oil and the lemon juice.

Note: Feel comfortable using frozen peas rather than out-of-season old woody ones, and if you like a bit of a kick, add ½ teaspoon chilli flakes with the anchovies and salt.

Sweet onion relish

1 small onion, cut into 1.5 cm (⅝ inch) thick wedges
splash of olive oil
45 ml (1½ fl oz) cider vinegar
2 teaspoons brown sugar
2 vine-ripened tomatoes, peeled and roughly chopped
    (page 19)
2 tablespoons caster (superfine) sugar
juice of 1 lemon

Serves 4

To make the relish, heat the oil in a large heavy-based saucepan and add the onion. Cook, stirring over low heat for about 15 minutes, or until the onion is very soft. Add the vinegar and brown sugar and cook, stirring often, for another 15 minutes, or until the mixture is lightly browned. Add the tomato, sugar and lemon juice to the pan, and stir over low heat until the sugar has dissolved, without letting it come to the boil. Increase the heat and simmer, uncovered, stirring occasionally, for about 40 minutes, or until the mixture thickens. Check the seasoning. Be careful that the relish doesn't stick to the bottom of the pan. Set aside to cool slightly, then refrigerate until needed. Serve at room temperature.

Potato salad

I have a few favourites when it comes to potato salad … but in a nutshell … I suggest you use beautiful small potatoes that are sweet and waxy such as kipflers (fingerling), bintjes (yellow finn) or pink eyes. I cook them with the skin on because I love the texture, but also because there are plenty of vitamins in the skin that are good for us. If the potatoes are bigger than you had hoped for, they can always be sliced after cooking, but keep that skin on.

About 100 g (3½ oz) potato per person is generally enough. Simply wash them well, simmer in a saucepan of salted water until they are tender, then drain. While they are still warm, crush them slightly with a potato masher and drizzle with extra virgin olive oil, red wine vinegar, sea salt and freshly ground pepper. The warm potatoes will soak up the liquids beautifully, so add a touch more dressing when serving, along with a sprinkling of fresh herbs.

Another dressing idea would be to sauté some bacon, onion and garlic, finishing it with the extra virgin olive oil and red wine vinegar, or you could make a delicious creamy yoghurt mixture with finely chopped garlic … or aïoli (page 246) … the options are endless.

Potato gratin

500 g (1 lb 2 oz) bintje (yellow finn) or other waxy
   potatoes
250 ml (9 fl oz/1 cup) cream (whipping)
sea salt and freshly ground pepper
20 g (¾ oz) unsalted butter, melted

Serves 4–6

Peel and cut the potatoes into 2 mm (1/16 inch) thick slices, covering the slices with the cream to prevent discolouration. Season the potato slices with sea salt and freshly ground pepper. Brush the base and sides of a shallow baking tray or gratin dish with the melted butter. Remove the potato slices from the cream and overlap them in lines down the dish until about 2–3 cm (¾ –1¼ inches) deep. If using a round dish, put the slices down in a circle and cover the middle with another circle of potato. Drizzle a little cream between each layer. Pour any remaining cream over. Bake at 180°C (350°F/Gas 4) for 50–60 minutes, or until lightly browned and tender.

When done, cut the gratin into four or six portions and place on the plate next to your meat or serve in the dish in the middle of the table. Don't forget that the gratin can be made in advance and reheated.

Roast potatoes

700 g (1 lb 9 oz) bintje (yellow finn), pink eye or kipfler
    (fingerling) potatoes, peeled and cut into large
    pieces, or left whole if small
sea salt
2 tablespoons extra virgin olive oil
freshly ground pepper

Serves 4

Preheat the oven to 200°C (400°F/Gas 6). Put the potatoes in a saucepan of cold water, add some sea salt and place over high heat for 10–12 minutes. The potato should still be slightly hard in the middle when drained. Allow the potato to cool for a few minutes, then put in a bowl with the oil and toss to combine. Spread the potato out in a roasting tin and roast for 20 minutes, turning every 5 minutes to ensure an even golden brown colour (the time needed will vary depending on the variety used).

To check the potato is done, pierce one with a small knife. It will glide in easily when it is cooked through. When the potato is crisp, sprinkle with sea salt and freshly ground pepper. Either place beside the meat, poultry or fish on individual plates or serve in the middle of the table.

Note: I'm sure I don't need to tell you that the addition of yam or pumpkin (winter squash), parsnip, Jerusalem artichokes and various other root vegetables can only enhance the modest roast spud.

Potato chips

Waxy potatoes such as bintje (yellow finn) make great chips (fries) and, as with roast potatoes, the trick is double cooking. Peel and cut your potatoes into thick slices, then cut the slices into chips about 1 cm (1/2 inch) wide. Give them a good wash in cold water to help remove some of the starch. Wrap in a tea towel (dish towel) to dry and make sure you remove all the moisture, or you will have spitting chips, which is where the saying comes from, I guess. Blanch the chips in batches in a large saucepan of hot oil (or in a deep-fryer) using a thermometer to get a temperature of about 170°C (325°F). Cook for 5 minutes without browning, then drain on paper towel. Increase the temperature to 190°C (375°F) and cook the chips in batches until they are golden brown. Drain again on

paper towel. Just before serving, sprinkle the chips liberally with sea salt.

You can of course turn your chips into French fries with a little handy knife work. Once you taste home-made fries it is really hard to go back to the mass-produced ones that are not 100 per cent potato. Remember that keeping the oil temperature constant is the secret to success with deep-frying; also don't be tempted to overfill the pan or fryer. Do the chips in batches and keep the cooked ones warm in the oven.

Potato purée

600 g (1 lb 5 oz) bintje (yellow finn) or other waxy
    potatoes, peeled and cut into 2–3 cm (^{3}/4–1^{1}/4 inch)
    dice
5 garlic cloves
sea salt
150 ml (5 fl oz) milk, warmed
150 g (5^{1}/2 oz) unsalted butter, finely diced
freshly ground pepper
juice of ^{1}/2 lemon

Serves 4

Put the potato in a bamboo steamer. Add the garlic and steam over a saucepan of boiling water for about 1 hour, or until the potato is cooked. When done, pass the potato and garlic through a food mill or potato ricer. Put the potato and garlic in a saucepan over medium heat and stir with a wooden spoon for 1 minute until the potato begins to steam. Add a little sea salt and, while stirring continuously, pour in the warm milk. Add the butter a bit at a time, stirring until it has fully incorporated and the purée is smooth. Give a good grind of pepper, check the amount of salt, add the lemon juice to the purée and stir through. It is now ready to serve and if you want to go the extra mile, push it through a sieve. You won't be disappointed with the results.

Soft polenta

250 g (9 oz/1^{2}/3 cups) good-quality 'real' polenta
sea salt
100 g (3^{1}/2 oz/heaped ^{1}/3 cup) unsalted butter, chopped
150 g (5^{1}/2 oz/1^{1}/2 cups) finely grated Parmesan
freshly ground pepper

Serves 4

Bring 1.25–1.5 litres (44–52 fl oz/5–6 cups) water to the boil in a saucepan. Add some sea salt and pour in the polenta, whisking constantly, until it is completely incorporated. Reduce the heat and cook for 40 minutes at a gentle simmer, stirring from time to time with a wooden spoon. Stir in the butter and Parmesan, check for saltiness and give a good grind of pepper. The polenta is now ready to serve.

Steamed jasmine rice

500 g (1 lb 2 oz/2$\frac{1}{2}$ cups) jasmine rice

Serves 4

Put the rice in a small saucepan and rinse two or three times by running cold water over it to cover, then pouring the water out. This rids the rice of excess starch powder and of any broken rice that will make the cooked rice mushy and sticky. Add just enough water — about 750 ml (26 fl oz/3 cups) — to cover the top of the rice by 1 cm (1/2 inch). A convenient trick is to touch the top of the rice in the pan with your middle finger. The water level should be just below the first joint of your finger. No further measuring needed.

Cover the pan with the lid. Put over medium to medium–high heat and bring to the boil. Immediately reduce the heat to low. Simmer, covered, for another 10 minutes, or until the water has all evaporated. Turn off the heat and allow the rice to sit, covered, for at least a further 5 minutes. Serve hot or at room temperature. Fluff with a fork before serving.

Couscous

3 tablespoons olive oil
500 g (1 lb 2 oz/2$\frac{1}{2}$ cups) instant couscous

Serves 4–6

Combine the oil and 500 ml (17 fl oz/2 cups) boiling water in a large bowl. Gradually stir the couscous into the water. Fluff the couscous with a fork, then transfer it to a muslin-lined steamer, and steam for about 20 minutes, or until tender and cooked through.

Harissa

8 dried long red chillies, soaked overnight in water
1 teaspoon ground cumin
1 teaspoon ground coriander
4 garlic cloves
1 teaspoon sea salt
80 ml (2½ fl oz/⅓ cup) olive oil

Makes about 125 ml (4 fl oz/½ cup)

Drain the chillies and reserve 2 tablespoons of the soaking water. Cut the stems off the tops of the chillies and roughly chop the flesh. Blend all the ingredients, including the reserved soaking water, until you form a rough paste. Use immediately or spoon into a sterilised jar, cover with a thin layer of oil, seal and refrigerate until needed.

Chicken stock

1.6 kg (3 lb 8 oz) corn-fed chicken

Makes about 2.5 litres (87 fl oz/10 cups)

Wash the chicken and remove the fat from the cavity. Set the chicken on a chopping board and with a large cook's knife or a cleaver cut off the legs at the point where the thigh and drumstick meet. Make a few slashes into the flesh with a sharp knife. Cut the wings off where they meet the breast, then cut down the side of the chicken so the back comes off the breast. Cut the back and breast in half, and again, cut into the flesh slightly.

Put 3 litres (105 fl oz/12 cups) water in a large saucepan and add the chicken pieces. Bring to the boil, then reduce the heat to the barest simmer and cook, uncovered, for about 4 hours. Remove any impurities from the surface during the cooking process. Carefully strain the stock twice through fine strainer lined with muslin (cheesecloth) and discard the chicken pieces. Cool to room temperature, then refrigerate; remove he layer of fat before using.

This will last up to 4 days in the refrigerator.

Classic mayonnaise

3 egg yolks
sea salt
2 tablespoons lemon juice
375 ml (13 fl oz/1½ cups) half olive oil, half extra
    virgin olive oil
freshly ground pepper

Makes about 400 ml (14 fl oz)

Put a saucepan large enough to hold a stainless steel bowl on a bench. Place a tea towel (dish towel) around the inside edge of the pan and place the bowl on top; this will hold the bowl steady while you whisk.

Put the eggs in the bowl and whisk. Add the sea salt and lemon juice and, while whisking, drizzle in the oil very slowly. As the emulsion starts to form, add the oil in a steady stream. Don't let the oil sit on the surface as this can cause the mayonnaise to split. Add a grind of pepper and check for salt and lemon juice.

Serve immediately or keep in the refrigerator for up to 1 week.

Aïoli

3 egg yolks
3–4 garlic cloves, crushed
sea salt
2 tablespoons lemon juice
375 ml (13 fl oz/1½ cups) half olive oil, half extra
    virgin olive oil
sea salt and freshly ground pepper

Makes about 400 ml (14 fl oz)

Put a saucepan large enough to hold a stainless steel bowl on a bench. Place a tea towel (dish towel) around the inside edge of the pan and place the bowl on top; this will hold the bowl steady while you whisk.

Put the egg yolks in the bowl and whisk. Add the garlic, sea salt and lemon juice and, while whisking, drizzle in the oil very slowly. As the emulsion starts to form, add the oil in a steady stream. Don't let the oil sit on the surface as this can cause the aïoli to split. Add a grind of pepper and check the seasoning for salt and lemon juice.

Serve immediately or keep in the refrigerator for up to 1 week.

Béarnaise

2 French shallots, sliced
2 tarragon sprigs
5 whole black peppercorns
125 ml (4 fl oz/$\frac{1}{2}$ cup) white wine
125 ml (4 fl oz/$\frac{1}{2}$ cup) tarragon vinegar
3 egg yolks
250 g (9 oz) unsalted butter, cut into cubes, then
    brought to room temperature
2 tablespoons chopped tarragon

Makes about 250 ml (9 fl oz/1 cup)

Put the shallots, tarragon, peppercorns, wine and vinegar into a saucepan. Heat over medium–high heat and reduce until 80 ml (2$\frac{1}{2}$ fl oz/$\frac{1}{3}$ cup) remains. Put the egg yolks in a bowl that will sit comfortably over a saucepan. Strain the tarragon reduction and pour over the egg yolks, whisking to incorporate. Put the bowl over a saucepan of barely simmering water and start whisking. As it approaches the point at which it is fully cooked, the mixture will thicken by doubling or tripling in size. Once the sauce is thick, start adding three to four cubes of butter at a time, whisking to incorporate. When all the butter is incorporated, remove the bowl from the heat, add the chopped tarragon and check the seasoning.

Acknowledgements

This little book has been a collaboration of the usual suspects, so I would like to thank them all for their efforts.

Firstly, my great team of trusted wonderful cooks, who for some reason have decided that a nine-to-five job is more to their liking. That works for me — and they get weekends off. Without them, finishing these projects would be impossible: Sarah Swan, head organiser and 'can't live without' member of the team; David Young, ex-Rockpool and handy as a great all-rounder; and Jess Sly, who gives us a great insight into how the non-professional cook approaches these recipes, invaluable for making them foolproof.

Kay Scarlett, my publisher. Though I'm not quite sure how she talked me into this one, I'm pleased she did.

The whole team at Murdoch — you are a dream to work with. Thanks for putting up with all the changes, but you now know how I like to evolve these things, so big thanks to Janine Flew, Margaret Malone, Marylouise Brammer and Sarah Odgers.

Sue Fairlie-Cuninghame and Earl Carter — I love putting the team back together, and these book shoots are among the highlights of the year. Both of you are dear friends, and importantly the fuel which keeps me going with all the mad projects I take on. Thank you, thank you, thank you for being there and being my inspiration.

Very importantly, thanks to my beautiful children, Josephine, Macy and Indy, who make life richer — I hope you will cook from this book.

I guess the biggest thanks need to go to my beautiful wife, Samantha, for knowing these books mean less time with the family and a little more stress in my life; still she puts up with it. You really do make it all possible and worthwhile.

Index

Published in 2007 by Murdoch Books Pty Limited
www.murdochbooks.com.au

Murdoch Books Australia
Pier 8/9
23 Hickson Road
Millers Point NSW 2000
Phone: +61 (0) 2 8220 2000
Fax: +61 (0) 2 8220 2558

Murdoch Books UK Limited
Erico House
6th Floor
93–99 Upper Richmond Road
Putney, London SW15 2TG
Phone: +44 (0) 20 8785 5995
Fax: +44 (0) 20 8785 5985

Chief Executive: Juliet Rogers
Publishing Director: Kay Scarlett

Project manager: Janine Flew
Editor: Margaret Malone
Concept and design: Marylouise Brammer
Design: Sarah Odgers
Photographer: Earl Carter
Stylist and art director: Sue Fairlie-Cuninghame
Production: Maiya Levitch
Assistants to Neil Perry and food preparation: Sarah
     Swan, Jessica Sly

National Library of Australia Cataloguing-in-Publication Data
   Perry, Neil, 1957– . Good food. Includes index.
   ISBN 9781740459235. ISBN 1 74045 923 7.
   1. Quick and easy cookery. I. Title. 641.5

Colour reproduction by Splitting Image Colour Studio, Melbourne, Australia.

Printed by i-Book Printing Ltd in 2007. PRINTED IN CHINA.

The Publisher and Neil Perry would like to thank the following for the use of their merchandise in the photography of this book: Aeria Country Floors, Woollahra, NSW; All Handmade Gallery, Waverley, NSW; Camargue, Mosman, NSW; Chefs Warehouse, Surry Hills, NSW; Francalia, Balgowlah, NSW; Honey Bee Homewares, Fairlight, NSW; Ici Et La, Surry Hills, NSW; In Residence, Northbridge, NSW; Lucienne Linen, Mosman, NSW; Malcolm Greenwood, Cremorne, NSW; Mud Australia, Marrickville, NSW; Ondene, Double Bay, NSW; Papaya, Bondi Junction, NSW; Parterre Garden, Woollahra, NSW; Space Furniture, Alexandria, NSW; Studio Imports, Oakley, Vic; Staub Cookware, Port Air, NSW; The Bay Tree, Woollahra, NSW.

IMPORTANT: Those who might be at risk from the effects of salmonella poisoning (the elderly, pregnant women, young children and those suffering from immune deficiency diseases) should consult their doctor with any concerns about eating raw eggs.

CONVERSION GUIDE: You may find cooking times vary depending on the oven you are using. For fan-forced ovens, as a general rule, set the oven temperature to 20°C (35°F) lower than indicated in the recipe. We have used 20 ml (4 teaspoon) tablespoon measures. If you are using a 15 ml (3 teaspoon) tablespoon, for most recipes the difference will not be noticeable. However, for recipes using baking powder, gelatine, bicarbonate of soda (baking soda), small amounts of flour and cornflour (cornstarch), add an extra teaspoon for each tablespoon specified.